The Fool
&
The Mirror

by Julian Vayne

The Universe Machine

ISBN number 978-0-9954904-9-9

First published in December, 2018 by The Universe Machine, Norwich.

Books by the same author:

Seeds of Magick (with Catherine Summers)
The Inner Space Workbook (with Catherine Summers)
Personal Development with the Tarot (with Catherine Summers)
Pharmakon: Drugs and the Imagination
Now That's What I Call Chaos Magick (with Greg Humphries)
Magick Works: Stories of occultism in theory and practice
The Book of Baphomet (with Nikki Wyrd)
Wonderful Things: Learning with Museum Objects
Deep Magic Begins Here: Tales and Techniques of Practical Occultism
Chaos Craft (with Steve Dee)
Getting Higher: The Manual of Psychedelic Ceremony
Walking Backwards or, The Magical Art of Psychedelic Psychogeography (with Greg Humphries)

theblogofbaphomet.com

Dedication

This book is dedicated to my dear friends, those I know in person and those that I have met online. Thank you for your encouragement, love and support. May you be blessed.

Contents

Mirror Writing 1

Spirits, you are here! 5

The Fool and The Mirror: Concerning the Relations between Art, Magic & the Academy 17

From the Vasty Deep: The reality of DMT entities and other spirits 29

Mindfulness in the Museum 39

Stoned Temple Pilots: Set, Setting and Substance in Contemporary Entheogenic Spirituality 49

Through the Looking-Glass 61

The Typology of Magick 71

The Sun is Eclipsed by the Moon 77

Walking in the Silence of Spring 83

My First Trip 87

Enchant Long 95

Season of the Spiders 101

On Having a Girl's Aura 105

Tripping Out: Towards a Psychedelic Psychogeography 111

All Shall be Well 127

For Every Complex Problem... 133

Intent, Consequences and Virtue 137

Finding Your Way in the Woods: The Art of Greg Humphries 143

Children in the Circle: Paganism, Spirituality and our Families 161

Inspiration from the Darkness: The Psychology of Magick 165

On Being a Priest 171

Psychedelic Ceremony in Theory and Practice 175

Magick—Contains Mild Peril 187

The Art of Witchcraft 191

The Magic of St Nectan's Glen 205

Orange Sunshine 213

"In all chaos there is a cosmos,
in all disorder a secret order."

Carl Jung

Mirror Writing

This is the third collection of essays I've written; the first was *Magick Works* (2008) followed in 2013 by *Deep Magic Begins Here...* This book, like those earlier volumes, includes material from a variety of sources; previous unpublished writing as well re-worked and expanded texts first released in collections or journals.

The Fool and the Mirror includes thoroughly revised essays that were first presented on my blog, theblogofbaphomet.com. Established in 2011, this was the cauldron in which my 2015 collaboration with Steve Dee, *Chaos Craft: The Wheel of the Year in Eight Colours,* was brewed up. It has also been a space for writing which gave rise to two solo volumes by Steve Dee; *A Gnostic's Progress* (2015) and *The Heretic's Journey* (2018).

As someone now in my 50th year I've seen the culture of 'Western esotericism' (to use the description favoured in academia) develop over four decades and can look back in the proverbial rear view mirror of my own writing on this subject. My first published work, written when I was just 14 years old, was an article on the relationship between the Left and Right Hand Paths of magic, which appeared in the British popular New Age magazine, Destiny. Through subsequent years I've written often—personal journals, essays, books, pagan 'zines, ritual texts, academic papers and more. Reflecting on this corpus of material I can easily discern the key motifs; landscape, queer identity, occult philosophy and politics, seasonal ritual, witchcraft, drugs...

Far more explicitly than the previous two collections, this volume adds 'art' to that list of themes. As a young man I studied graphic design, and through various professional roles, I've kept up my engagement with the dark arts of marketing, branding and advertising. Today I frequently work with fine art collections in museums and galleries, where I help people engage with the artworks they encounter in those locations. This makes me wonder about the parallels between so-called High Magic and Low Magic, and Fine verses Graphic Art...

This collection touches explicitly on visual art, both as a means to understand occulture (in the essay 'The Typology of Magic') and as an expression of esoteric practice ('The Art of Witchcraft'). Here, more than in any previous work, I've included examples of the visual art I produce, in addition to the descriptions of 'installations' (ceremonial spaces) and 'performances' (rituals) that are the usual subjects of my writing.

As part of this emphasis on artistic practice I'm pleased to include an interview with one of my oldest and dearest friends Greg Humphries. Greg and I co-wrote *Now That's What I Call Chaos Magick* in 2005 and this year *Walking Backwards or, The Magical Art of Psychedelic Psychogeography*. Greg is a skilled woodsman, artist and magician. Together we share a love of landscape, magic and altered states. In these pages you will find descriptions of psychedelic psychogeography ('Tripping Out') a practice that Greg and I developed together. There are other explorations of sacred landscape here too, in the essays 'Walking In the Silence of Spring' and 'The Magic of St Nectan's Glen'.

Here you will find articles addressing the role of paganism and occultism to our families ('Children in the Circle') and to wider culture ('On Being a Priest'). Other essays explore the relationship between psychology and occultism ('Inspiration from the Darkness') and there are several meditations on esoteric philosophy covering subjects as diverse as the cultivation of virtue, the ontological nature of spirits and more.

My own initiation into the psychedelic experience is recounted here ('My First Trip') alongside descriptions of entheogenic practice. This is a field I've been devoting much of my time to over the last decade or more, through my involvement in organizations such as Breaking Convention (the biennial conference on psychedelic consciousness), The Psychedelic Museum project and following the publication of my book *Getting Higher: The Manual of Psychedelic Ceremony.*

The Fool & The Mirror thus presents a multitude of reflections of occult practice. The collection takes its name from an essay which was written for the first journal of the Black Mirror Research group, an academic body that brings together scholarly research on the relationship between occultism and the arts.

There are many other mirrors in this book; in the pieces about gender and identity ('On Having A Girl's Aura' and 'Through the Looking Glass') as well as a literal black mirror ('The Sun is Eclipsed by the Moon'). The black scrying mirror mentioned in that essay appears on the cover of this book, and many of my own artworks reproduced here use mirrors in their creation.

Within this hall of mirrors, I hope that you will discover stories to entertain you, opportunities to reflect on your practice, and perhaps a little light to illuminate your own magical journey.

Let us step together through the looking-glass, darkly and into the world of the imagination and of magic...

Julian Vayne
Devon 2018

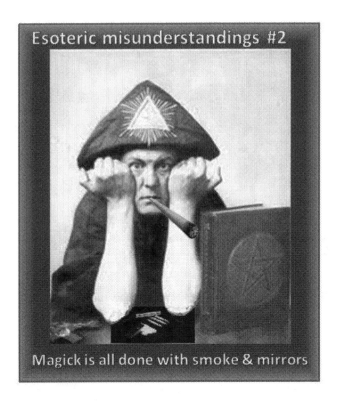

Beastly meme

Spirits, you are here!

An account written two days after a journey with 1P-LSD while exploring the effects of this material at a moderately high dose.

I am running, falling to the point of flying, down a steep sand dune. I am dressed in a black robe, my arms extended, each hand holding long black and white feathers, beaded, tied into ceremonial fans. The beadwork flashes red, blue, green, purple and a colour beyond sight. My hair streams out. There are feathers in my hair. There is the sound of rushing wind.

I see I am but one of a multitude of figures, each dressed alike, forming a line of descending chaos shamans, running down that hill. We are like a berserker army, crashing headlong towards an unseen plain, above us an intense clear sky. Then the vision changes and I am aware that each of us in this charging army are but barbs on the feathers of a fan. This fan is held by a gigantic shaman who is running down a hill, under the same bright blue sky. We are an infinite company who are no more than the tiniest part of a much greater form, a phalanx within one vast figure, who is itself part of another tumult of runners, and so on for eternity...

How did I get here?

The day began with a visit to a friend's land. A beautiful arboretum, in its first decade of growth. Exotic maples and Chinese bamboos festoon the valley at the bottom of which is a large pond. Above this oasis metallic damselflies and dragonflies zigzag through the sky. A water lily is open to the sun and innumerable tiny lives circulate both upon the meniscus and below the water-line.

Beneath the hot summer sun, we sit and talk. Rather than impose a ritual of our own devising on this magnificent space our intention is rather to listen to the landscape itself. We begin a mindful walk through the garden. We pause beside a grove of (baby) giant sequoia trees, touch their furry bark and embrace them. We follow the winding pathway through botanical rarities, sniffing the air and touching the inviting tubes of bamboo that clatter gently in the breeze. Clumps of hydrangeas (the diversity of which makes this a collection of national significance) glow an unexpected fluorescent purple-blue on the hillside.

Later, by the pool we sit and meditate, breathing in the sweet, warm air and begin to drum. Our three instruments sing in the air, the beats mixing with the wind, the buzzing of insects, the distant barking of dogs. In this manner we connect with and are nurtured by the landscape, we open ourselves to the space and are nourished by it. We hold hands, because that's always nice.

Returning home my intention is to perform an experiment. A strong dose of a new substance, a novel lysergamide that I have explored only at lower dose and in combination with other more familiar medicines.

Evening comes. I have prepared the space by banishing in the time-honoured manner of washing up, sweeping the floors, fumigation with cleansing incense, and setting new candles on my altar. The house is ready, as am I.

Taking the material, I swallow, asking for the protection and blessing of this spirit. It's time to go for a walk.

Leaving the building the sun is still up, though now it dips in its summertime pathway, far to the north-west. Swifts and gulls punctuate the sky. Light glints on the river as the tide drains the water through the groove that it has been carving since before the last ice age, across the land.

The first indications that something is happening occur in the wasteland. Concrete platforms, the remains of the old gasworks that once sat on the outskirts of town, have been overrun with buddleia, hedged around by hazel and brambles. Here ox-eye daisies stand in their hundreds like narrow citadels, their flowers are beginning to glow. Vetch snakes between them with its pea tendrils, the colour of its violet flowers has also been turned up by the medicine. I am one hour past drop time, in the early stages of a journey that is likely to last for some eight hours.

I am inspired to take a path I rarely walk, hopping over a farmer's gate. There is a huge oak tree. The fissures on its trunk are highlighted by the sun and by the sacrament within me. I ascend the sloping Devonian hill, rough pasture peppered with the occasional cow pat. Upon the summit I can sit and watch as the sun sets behind Spielbergian clouds, shooting out jets of yellow light. A huge wall of cloud moves slowly in from the south-west, bringing moist air and the promise of rain. It reminds me of a vast spacecraft from Close Encounters or Independence Day. The CGI in my mind has been enabled. The waxing moon stands pin-point clear in the softening blue, before skeins of white cloud catch upon its horns and obscure it from sight.

Walking down the hill there is a strange alertness in my body. Though I am alone here (the nearest people are a couple watching the sunset from the next hilltop down river from me) there is an ears-pricked-up attention in me. My endocrine glands are spiking me with a dash of adrenaline as the chemistry that I am undergoes both subtle (in terms of physiological effects) and radical (in terms of psychological impact) changes.

I walk back home, gathering flowers from the hedgerows as I do so. There is meadowsweet and ragwort, *Centranthus ruber* and *Chaerophyllum hirsutum* 'Roseum'. My practice is to keep flowers on my hearth altar and now, in the high summer, there are both blooms and the first setting seed pods; black-bronze nodules of Alexanders, and rust-red spikes of dock. Each form I collect has great beauty. This is something I would notice even without the drugs but the increase in visual acuity, and the faint beginnings of tracer visuals, serve to make me even more attentive than usual to the exquisite glory of these kerbside plants.

Entering my house, I place the bouquet into a jug. As I empty it to receive the fresh blooms, I realise I must move carefully. I'm holding a unique vessel made by a highly skilled local octogenarian potter who produces work in the traditional north Devon *sgraffito* style. This object is precious, and so I go into 'museum curator mode' using both hands, holding the jug not by its handle, but cradled in my palms. I remind myself that I don't need to rush. As a person who, generally, tends towards an impulsive, somewhat speedy style, I remember that I should pay attention to this moment rather than focusing all my attention on getting the job done in order to do something else. I'm attentive to the design on the vessel; a prayer or spell is written there, taken from a public monument erected in a West Country city which, unbeknownst to many, was funded by a local coven of witches. The jug's incised design includes a vèvè of Pomba Gira and a slightly saucy depiction of the Bideford Witches, some of the last people to be hanged in England for the crime of witchcraft.

Potted history

Back in the living room I light the candles. The sun has set but the long summer twilight lingers, even with the gathering clouds. Energy rushes, similar to those I sometimes get on psilocybin mushrooms, skitter through my body. I do a few yoga moves to release and relax but I don't want to stop these increasingly vibrant sensations, they are interesting and pleasurable. Yes, I'm definitely tripping now.

I lay down under a blanket, the smoke from an incense stick curls in the light of the candle flame. I put on Departure Songs by Hammock. This isn't an album I know but I trust my friend's recommendation and so I start my journey to the sound of post-prog rock guitars, sweeping across a backdrop of digital sounds. I like to have examples of both familiar and novel music in the playlist when I'm tripping.

The bodily twitching increases and I go with it. Like shaking trance, seething seiðr to some, quaking and quivering, I can feel these ripples of energy moving through me. Some spasms break out of my wrists and ankles, I imagine that the medicine is acting like an internal chiropractor, manipulating my energy body and shaking out all the kinks and restrictions.

Later as the peak builds, I am dancing, the music is different now, tribal-trance-techno rhythms. Night-time has fallen and outside the rain and wind have arrived.

There is a moment when I'm standing in the centre of the room, a distinct feeling of a hand being placed upon my right shoulder; I exclaim aloud, 'spirits, you are here!'. This is a clear tactile sensation and, although when I look there is no visual evidence of a presence, to the inner eye it is obvious that I am standing in a circle of friends. Our arms are round each other's shoulders and we are aware that, just as we have our individual minds, we are also one mind. We are focused on a form, a morphing vision which, though connected to the music is arising independently from it. Here the shape is a felt sensation. There is a synaesthesia of the kinaesthetic sense, such that the forms in my mind arise not as colourful morphing visions, but as felt geometric relationships. What some call an 8B geometry emerges; a sense that all possible points in space and time are perceived as an embodied, yet somehow still 'visual' network of relationships. These visions come together in one key-stone event, erecting a self-perceiving architecture of the moment that unites all opposites, and sets my awareness as both the diamond-pointed jewel in the heart of this marvellous lotus, and simultaneously the circumference at the uttermost edge of the universe. A vision emerges as the embodied experience of rushing forward under a bright blue sky.

Then I am running down a hill, holding feathers...

Gradually, over hours, the intensity diminishes and while with open eyes the world is brighter, and more detailed, I can feel that the medicine has peaked and is slowly on the wane. I start reflecting on the experience; for me this behaviour clearly signals that the trip is over and I'm coming in to land.

I check my email and social media feeds. A petition calling for the legalisation of cannabis use in Britain has just been launched which earlier in the evening I'd been sharing across my network. The number of signatures has jumped by tens of thousands and is going up at a rate of knots. I make a reefer with the last of my tobacco and smoke it. As I do so I fix my intention, that this petition will exceed 100,000 signatures, which is the point at which the government with consider discussing an issue. I resolve not to smoke tobacco after this, until the debate is had. The last waft of spliff smoke, sending my spell up towards the ever-dancing form of the Shiva Nataraja on my hearth altar. I state my purpose aloud, choosing my words with care, and burn the last part of the joint in a ritual offering bowl, beneath the form of the dancing ecstatic god.

The dawn brings rain. I extinguish the candles and pull on my walking boots. Crossing the medieval bridge as the cloud occluded sun begins to rise, I take a familiar path down by the river but then, noticing that the tide is pulling back, exposing slippery mudflats and yellow sand, I decide on a new direction, a way I'd never walked before, a new way, downstream and along the west bank. That curious chemical cascade that the lysergamides initiate is entering its last phase. There is no immaculate sunny morning to enjoy; the air is wet though warm, with falling curtains of rain buffeted along by a strong wind. But the sun is in ascendancy and cracks of blue appear as I pick my way along the slippery seaweed-covered shore. In this afterglow time, the world is made new. Everything is revealed in the symbolic power of being deeply itself. The commonplace, one is reminded, is sacred. Egrets, European incarnations of wise Thoth, stride along the waterline and take to the air. In the river mud there are the tiny noises of living things. The trees breathe out the air that I breathe in.

I near the gothic archways of an ancient lime kiln, to the untrained eye a structure that looks like a ruined castle folly. I am transfixed by the curving stonework. There is rabbit close-cropped grass that is an astonishing, vibrant green around this workaday riverside architectural artwork. I shelter from the rain and, when the sky clears, make my way back along the path. Back across the iron bridge, over the turbulent river, and home.

There I meditate, take a bath and sleep, perchance to dream.

For some people their engagement with psychoactives is an occasional experience, or perhaps something they did when younger but no longer. For those of us with an ongoing relationship with these substances there are several things that keep us coming back for more. One attraction is that new chemicals, new entheogens, provide a range of subtly different windows onto the world, in both its inner and outer manifestations. Some materials produce kaleidoscopic visions and optically perceived narratives. Other substances modify our kinaesthetic senses, others will affect smell and taste. Though psychedelic substances may affect specific aspects of the sensorium, they act on the whole self; the totality of our awareness dwells within each state.

Along with the range of effects from different drugs there is also the fact that one cannot, as they say, step into the same river twice. Each time we take a psychedelic substance, even if it is one we have taken before, we do so from the unique set and setting in which we find ourselves. A trip is always different because it always happens to a different person; for we are a flow, an enacted process and not a fixed 'I'. Thus, insights gained from a successfully managed psychedelic experience are always novel.

Psychedelics have an introspective and healing power. During the journey described above I encountered lots of personal psychological stuff, the kind of wounds and issues that we all accumulate, as humans living in the world. We acquire these hurts, perhaps as a result of specific trauma, or sometimes just through the wear and tear of life.

We know from contemporary research and innumerable testimonies from users that psychedelic substances can be good medicines for people seeking to address post-traumatic stress disorder and a range of other mental health issues. For those of us who are not 'ill' psychedelics act as a tonic for our awareness, an enema that helps flush out the suffering that comes with being human, allowing us to see things from a new vantage point. For those for whom this method works, psychedelics allow a self-led psychoanalysis, a tool for inner-exploration that engenders healing and wholeness.

There is also the fact that, though the psychedelic experience can be challenging, it is potentially joyful, even ecstatic or numinous. We have a strange relationship with pleasure in Western culture. On the one hand the 'pursuit of happiness' is considered a legitimate driver for our actions, and yet to take pleasure in our use of drugs is often imagined to be morally wrong.

For example; while the medical use of cannabis might be tolerated, the idea that cannabis might be pleasurable in itself can be seen as a problem by some; Sometimes these feelings are understandably rationalized as being rooted in the fear of addiction and the suffering that can cause. However, Euro-American culture is deeply anti-euphoric, to use a term culled from the excellent *Marijuana Revolution* by John Sinclair. In contrast to this, medicine information sheets do not list enjoyable side effects. I believe that the recreational, 're-creational', use of psychedelic substance is another reason to change the laws governing their use.

Many other animals besides humans like getting high, we're not alone in our desire to enjoy drugs. That's why I'd like to see post-prohibition policies that actually address this 'human given' rather than attempting to prohibit it, causing so much hurt in the process. While, legalisation or decriminalisation of drugs won't fix all those drug related issues, addiction, crime and the rest. Nevertheless, it would allow us to manage those problems better, to maximise the benefits and mitigate the risks of getting high, more successfully than under prohibition. And while the legitimate medical use of psychedelic substances is an essential tactic in reintroducing them into Western culture, the deeper transformation will be for us to allow their use for both spiritual and recreational purposes.

There is a line taken from the work of Aleister Crowley in Wiccan liturgy—The Charge of the Goddess—that says, "all acts of love and pleasure are my rituals". Allowing for the usual caveats of not harming others and being sensitive to issues of context and consent, perhaps one day we will be able to take these substances because they are fun and because we love the pleasure they can give us. That would fit with my reading of both the Pagan and Thelemic ethic expressed in that text. Those who are apt to segregate the sacred and profane may find this suggestion shocking. However, a close look at the ethnography of even ultra-spiritual drugs like ayahuasca shows that in some 'native' cultures the brew is taken because people enjoy the visions; 'jungle TV' it's sometimes called.

The po-faced post-Protestantism of Western culture finds this attitude hard to handle, instead insisting on divisions between the spiritual, the recreational, the difficult and the enjoyable, between work and play. But psychedelics can be all these things. Maybe we can accept that psychedelic drugs engender experiences of delight, joy and ecstasy and that this is both healing and morally okay. Then we will have transformed our fraught relationship with these magical molecules and know it's not a sin to alter our awareness, and it's not a sin to enjoy being high.

Shamanic mask of 1P-LSD 300 μg

The Fool and The Mirror:
Concerning the Relations between Art, Magic & the Academy

Black Mirror *is a research network based at Arts University Bournemouth that explores the role of spirituality in contemporary art. In 2014 their eponymous journal was launched. This article appeared in the first volume numbered 0. In it I refer to the* Visions of Enchantment *Conference held at the University of Cambridge in the same year.*

This first volume of *Black Mirror* is numbered zero, rather than one: a suitable beginning for a series such as this. Zero is the number typically inscribed on the tarot card The Fool. The Fool, the first of the twenty-two trump cards, is a complex symbol. Zero itself is a 'vital absence', a nothing, without which both mathematics and mysticism are rather tricky.[i] So while Roman numerals suffice for the other twenty-one trumps of the tarot Major Arcana, the Fool stands outside this scheme, numbered with a digit that represents something in a sense before the alpha-to-omega series of archetypes expressed in the trumps that follow it. Zero is an arcane glyph, perhaps originating in the mysterious East, which we Europeans depict as a circle with no beginning and no end. An infinite shape, an ouroboros swallowing its own tail.

The zero is the great mystery, the attempt to express the inexpressible. It is perhaps no accident that at the same time the tarot enters Western history, so does the zero enter common usage in European culture. The zero symbol was used as a secret sign for decades after to represent mystery, while the word itself comes from the same etymological root as the verb 'decipher'.[ii]

In some renditions the Fool carries over his shoulder a bindle or knapsack, which some artists, notably Frieda Harris in her collaboration with Aleister Crowley on the Thoth Tarot, show stuffed with the ten pentacles or coins that appear on the final card of the deck, the Ten of Disks. In this way the iconography of the tarot recalls the notion that the cards represent the cyclical passage of 'the Fool's Journey'.[iii] Our foolish zero-hero sets out along the path of illumination and transformation, an exploration of the arcane mysteries, with key experiences represented by the twenty-one trumps and fifty-six suit cards of the deck.

In a sense this trump [The Fool] is like an introduction and preface to the 'book' that is the Tarot. As such, it has accumulated the most conceptual content of all the cards and the connections among these concepts form the ground upon which the figures of the 21 following trumps are perceived. In its symbols and images are the latent forms of many of the other trumps.[iv]

The Fool is also the only trump to have escaped the confines of the tarot and sneaked into standard Anglophone gaming decks as the Joker in the pack. Drenched in polysemous imagery, paradox and play, the Fool is a wandering stranger, perhaps imbued with some type of crazy wisdom.

Like the Fool, *Black Mirror* steps off into the unknown. Into territory we know as magic, occultism, the esoteric. This is the hidden world of sorcerers, mystics and charlatans; but even more arcane than the world of magic is the world of art. While we might say that occultism is the study of 'that which is hidden', the word 'art' resists definition with a Taoist level of inscrutability. In addition, like the Fool we carry with us a knapsack of coins: the hard-won gold of academic respectability, the techniques of citation, peer review and critical research.

For myself, I wonder if, like the Fool, I am also beginning a journey, stepping like Alice beyond my usual territory of esoteric writing, through this *Black Mirror*, into a new world.

As someone outside academia I've already crossed a boundary at *Black Mirror*'s inaugural conference held at the University of Cambridge in March 2014. There I found myself speaking with one of the academics present. 'Are you presenting a paper here?' she asked my partner and me. 'No,' I answered, 'we're occultists'. Strange how representing myself as a magician in that context feels like a confession, disclosing something intimate, maybe a little bit crazy. Yet here we are at a conference called Visions of Enchantment: Occultism, Spirituality & Visual Culture: clearly this is in some sense a magical event, but is it an event *for* magicians? Indeed, is *Black Mirror* a space where academic discourse can sit side by side with writing from esoteric practitioners or even artists?

'My name is Julian Vayne and I am an occultist!' feels like a declaration from Alcoholics Anonymous. Does my position as a practitioner here make me vulnerable? While occultism in the modern age, especially since what Kenneth Grant called the 'magical revival' of the twentieth century, is an acceptable if rather outré academic interest, actually being a (tarot) card-carrying practitioner: is that okay?[v]

I attended Visions of Enchantment because I am interested in the subjects of art and magic, because I had not visited Cambridge before, and because I knew a number of the people taking part as both delegates and speakers. But there was still that small moment of hesitation as I owned my identity as an occultist in that context.

I am also an artist: I work in media to express this magical sensibility as something we can call art. Since magic itself is often defined as both a 'Science and Art', it's unsurprising that many occultists are artists too.[vi] In my case this includes my writing: books, contributions to journals, and my blog (theblogofbaphomet.com). Much of what I write, like this article, is about my own journey—expressing my engagement with magic through personal narrative and sharing it with others.

It was through my writing that my magic practice first made contact with academia. Professor Ronald Hutton played no small role in this process. He invited me to speak with students at Bristol University (at the time I had authored several texts on Wicca, tarot and magic and was running a monthly pagan newspaper, Pagan Voice). Later I was invited to speak there at a conference on the history of magic.[vii]

Since that time my magician's writing has been included in several academic publications, notably *The New Generation Witches* (2007) and *Seeking the Sacred with*

Psychoactive Substances (2014). My relationship with the academy is why I'm here, perhaps like a Fool, professing my practitioner status, a witch regarding himself in this *Black Mirror.*

My other art is as a practitioner of magic. Alone and with others I perform esoteric rites, and sometimes these are clearly 'art'. In decorated temple spaces, what in other contexts could be called 'installations', I write ceremonial poetry, make trance-inducing music, sing, make ritual gestures, blend incenses, deploy film and digital artefacts: all this and more is what my occultism looks like (or perhaps this is better expressed as being my 'witch's craft'). But this ritual art is, for the most part, hidden. It appears in the 'temporal autonomous zone': the pagan sacred space, the temple.[viii] It sometimes leaves traces as objects or photographs or the lingering scent of opopanax, but the true art itself (for me) is in the practice of the magic. What I do as a magician may throw off texts, ritual movements, chanted words of power and many other forms of either ephemeral or long-lived artefacts. Some of these find their way into the public sphere, although mostly they remain private.

For some magicians their art is a central expression and a primary vehicle for their magic. One such is Austin Spare, one of the first overtly esoteric artists to be positively re-evaluated by the English-speaking art world.[ix] One might argue that Spare should be a tutelary spirit of *Black Mirror.* I recall seeing his astonishing drawing 'The Dawn' at the Dark Monarch exhibition at Tate St Ives in 2009. There was the work of Spare, someone who I very much identified as part of my cultural tribe, a magician, with his art, his magic—radiant and powerful—in the heart of Tate. Alongside Spare's art were copies of British esoteric journals from the 1980s. Suddenly artefacts from my life, my culture, were being curated and shared in a world-class gallery.

This felt like the beginning of a cultural sea change of which *Black Mirror* is the latest stage. In the case of Austin Spare, not only could academia recognise he was a great artist but also that magic is the critical factor in his oeuvre. Without understanding 'Spare the magician' we cannot understand

'Spare the artist'. More recently Tate Modern acquired some art produced by the occultist and 'culture engineer' Genesis P-Orridge, art that also demands an understanding of the story of P-Orridge's occultism if we are to appreciate it fully.[x] Moreover, the occultism of these artists is no longer imagined as being pathological: this is not the naïve 'magical thinking' of Freud or the accommodation of madness that early anthropologists claimed shamanism represented.[xi] Rather this magic is a journey, an autopoietic technology, a way of exploring the mystery of existence, and the limits of our power.

My own identification as an occultist in the academic context also needs to be understood in terms of the broader history of scholarly engagement with esotericisms. Everyone wants to be taken seriously, for others to recognise them and appreciate the valuable contribution they make. For example, as an occultist I enjoy making the case that magical theory and practice have been critical in the development of many modern nuts-and-bolts innovations such as the telephone and the internet.[xii]

When academics first started looking at occultists, things didn't always work out well. For every sensitive analysis of the story of contemporary occultism (such as Margot Adler's *Drawing Down the Moon*) there have been other publications, sometimes derived from anthropological fieldwork, where informants have detected an underlying assumption that esoteric beliefs are simple self-deceptions. Such criticisms have been made, in personal communications to me, by people who were informants for Tanya Luhrmann's 1989 study of British esoteric culture *Persuasions of the Witch's Craft*. Thankfully the shortcomings that some informants perceived in Luhrmann's work have also been addressed by the academy: 'by not being upfront about her academic agenda with her subjects, Luhrmann's research had a serious negative impact on some of them, who claimed their traditions had been damaged by her releasing of initiate-only knowledge in published form'.[xiii]

Over the last decade or so I detect a cultural shift in the relationship of academia to occultism as a field of enquiry.

The establishment of the study of Western esotericism at the University of Amsterdam is emblematic of this change. It is also true to say that there are a goodly number of magicians, witches, pagans and others who now hold positions in both the sciences and humanities within academia. An even larger number of individuals have passed through the university system and had the opportunity to study esoteric matters in a way that treats them in their own terms, without the a priori assumption that the beliefs of magicians are in some way pathologically delusional.

Scholars, be they esoteric practitioners themselves or not, need to remain mindful that there are those within contemporary occultism who still view the interest of the academy with suspicion. Peter Grey, occultist, writer and co-founder of the esoteric publishing house Scarlet Imprint, says in a recent article entitled Rewilding Witchcraft: "How much have the elders [of witchcraft] sold us out, genuflecting to the academy ..." Grey suggests that there has been a 'compromise' as witchcraft and esoteric culture have made a bid for cultural acceptability. For him the increasing academic engagement with occultism is part of this process. He says; "the rise of Traditional Craft ... following the collapse of the Murray thesis and the disenchantment caused by Hutton's *Triumph of the Moon* ... whilst proposing a modern pagan witchcraft was, in retrospect, it's [Wicca's] death knell".[xiv]

While Grey sees academic engagement with occultism as an agent of Weberian disenchantment, there are others, including myself, who have a different reading of the situation. From the academy we have the work of scholars such as Christopher Partridge (*The Re-Enchantment of the West: Volume 1*, 2005) that challenges the idea of disenchantment being the dominant social process. At the coalface of academic esoteric research, we have seen the emergence of journals such as The Pomegranate and the Journal for the Academic Study of Magic, which include the voices of independent scholars who are often esoteric practitioners. This approach can go some way to addressing the concerns raised by Ronald Grimes: "Scholarly research is a form of hunting, predatory, even parasitic, upon whatever it studies. Things studied are soon deadened, rendered corpse like. Scholarship necessarily, not accidentally consumes what it studies", and by the writer and occultist Taylor Ellwood: "while academics would like to hold themselves above the idea of cultural appropriation, they are nonetheless very capable of it, as any history of anthropology will show".[xv]

My own hope is that *Black Mirror* can be a respectful as well as intellectually rigorous space where occultism (and its expression as art) is explored, critiqued and discussed by practitioners and non-practitioners alike. This can be done in a way that both respects the requirements of the academy and acknowledges esotericism as something more than a raw resource that can be mined to produce scholarly publications.

While *Black Mirror* represents part of the ongoing story of the relationship between the esoteric and the academic, there is also the relationship between art and magic to consider. As I alluded to above when considering my own practice in terms of art, there are ongoing discussions concerning the relationship of these practices within the contemporary esoteric community itself.

The magician and writer Alan Moore sees the arts and magic as natural allies:

Certainly, the arts have always treated magic with more sympathy and more respect than science (which, historically, has always sought to prove that occultists are fraudulent or else deluded) and religion (which, historically, has always sought to prove that occultists are flammable). While it shares the social standing and widespread respect afforded to the church or the laboratory, art as a field does not seek to exclude, nor is it governed by a doctrine that's inimical to magic, such as might be said of its two fellow indicators of humanity's cultural progress. After all, while magic has, in relatively recent times, produced few mighty theologians of much note and even fewer scientists, it has produced a wealth of inspired and inspiring painters, poets and musicians. Maybe we should stick with what we know we're good at?"

The advantages of treating magic as an art seem at first glance to be considerable. For one thing, there are no entrenched and vested interests capable of mounting an objection to magic's inclusion in the canon, even if they entertained objections in the first place, which is hardly likely. This is patently far from the case with either science or religion, which are by their very natures almost honour-bound to see that magic is reviled and ridiculed, marginalized and left to rust there on history's scrap-heap with the Flat Earth, water-memory and phlogiston. Art, as a category, represents a fertile and hospitable environment where magic's energy could be directed to its growth and progress as a field, rather than channelled into futile struggles for acceptance, or burned uselessly away by marking time to the repeated rituals of a previous century. Another benefit, of course, lies in art's numinosity, its very lack of hard-edged definition and therefore its flexibility. The questions 'what exactly are we doing and why are doing it', questions of 'method' and of 'aim', take on a different light when asked in terms of art. Art's only aim can be to lucidly express the human mind and heart and soul in all their countless variations, thus to further human culture's artful understanding of the universe and of itself, its growth towards the light. Art's method is whatever can be even distantly imagined. These parameters of purpose and procedure are sufficiently elastic, surely, to allow inclusion of magic's most radical or most conservative agendas? Vital and progressive occultism, beautifully expressed, that has no obligation to explain or justify itself. Each thought, each line, each image made exquisite for no other purpose than that they be offerings worthy of the gods, of art, of magic itself. The Art for The Art's sake.[xvi]

Moore isn't alone in holding the view that magic and art have much in common. Aleister Crowley wrote in *Magick in Theory and Practice*: "To conclude, one may add that natural artistic ability, if you possess it, forms an excellent guide. All Art is Magick"; and "There is no more potent means than Art of calling forth true Gods to visible appearance".[xvii]

Given the views of these two magician-artists, one might suggest that scholarly specialisms within the arts are likely to provide an optimum approach through which the academy can engage with magic.

Informed by the tradition of research and reflection, guided by an attitude of respect, inclusivity and daring (remember our Fool walking off the cliff into the unknown?), this *Black Mirror* can be held up to 'occulture' (a term coined by occultists themselves). Reflected in this looking glass are the images of magicians and of artists—perhaps even visions of people who are scholars *and* artists *and* occultists, challenging the notion that these need be separate, compartmentalised worlds.

Armed with our knapsack of golden coins, let us step together through this dark doorway, the hole in the zero, magically travelling through the surface of the mirror and into the mystery beyond. We may all learn something here...

Notes

i Lispector, *A Breath of Life*, p.3.
ii Janik, *Fools and Jesters*, p.457.
iii Pollack, *Seventy-Eight Degrees of Wisdom*, p.99.
iv Krakowski, *Ancient and Occult Genetic Code*.
v Grant, *The Magical Revival*.
vi Crowley, *The Book of Thoth*, p.131
vii Vayne, 'Two Worlds and In-between', p.81.
viii Bey, *T.A.Z.*
ix See among others Ansell, 'Austin Osman Spare: Biography'.
x Genesis P-Orridge, It's That Time Of The Month (from Tampax Romana) (1975), in the collection of Tate Modern, ref T13864.
xi Narby and Huxley (eds), *Shamans Through Time*.
xii Davis, *Techgnosis*.
xiii Wallis, 'Between the Worlds', p.205.
xiv Grey, 'Rewilding Witchcraft'.
xv Grimes, *Rite out of Place*, p.99; Ellwood, 'Academic Cultural Appropriation', p.114.
xvi Moore, 'Fossil Angels'.
xvii Crowley, *Magick in Theory and Practice* p.210.

References

Adler, Margot. *Drawing Down the Moon: Witches, Druids, Goddess-Worshippers, and Other Pagans in America Today*. New York: Viking Press, 1979
Ansell, Robert. 'Austin Osman Spare: Biography'. 2007. http://fulgur.co.uk/artists/austin-osman-spare/ (accessed 16 July 2014)
Bey, Hakim [Peter Lamborn Wilson]. *T.A.Z.: The Temporary Autonomous Zone. New York*: Autonomedia, 1991
Crowley, Aleister. *The Book of Thoth: A Short Essay on the Tarot of the Egyptians* [1944]. New York: Weiser, 1980
—. *Magick in Theory and Practice*. London: Routledge & Kegan Paul, 1983
— and Frieda Harris. *The Thoth Tarot*. Stamford, CT: U.S. Games, 2008
Davis, Erik. *Techgnosis: Myth, Magic and Mysticism in the Age of Information*. New York: Harmony Books, 1998
Ellwood, Taylor. 'Academic Cultural Appropriation of Neopaganism and Occultism'. In Lupa (ed.), *Talking About the Elephant*. Stafford: Megalithica Books, 2008
Grant, Kenneth. *The Magical Revival*. London: Frederick Muller, 1972
Grey, Peter. 'Rewilding Witchcraft'. 2014. http://scarletimprint.com/2014/06/rewilding-witchcraft/ (accessed 16 July 2014)

Grimes, Ronald L. *Rite out of Place: Ritual, Media, and the Arts.* New York: Oxford University Press, 2006

Hutton, Ronald. *The Triumph of the Moon: A History of Modern Pagan Witchcraft.* Oxford: Oxford University Press, 1999

Janik, Vicki K. *Fools and Jesters in Literature, Art, and History: A Bio-Bibliographical Sourcebook.* Westport, CT: Greenwood Press, 1998

Johnston, Hannah E., and Peg Aloi (eds). *The New Generation Witches: Teenage Witchcraft in Contemporary Culture.* Aldershot and Burlington, VT: Ashgate, 2007

Krakowski, Steve. An Ancient and Occult Genetic Code. 1996. http://www.bibliotecapleyades.net/ciencia/occultgeneticcode/tarot00.HTM (accessed 16 July 2014)

Lispector, Clarice. *A Breath of Life.* Tr. Johnny Lorenz. New York: New Directions Books, 2012

Luhrmann, Tanya. *Persuasions of the Witch's Craft.* Cambridge, MA: Harvard University Press, 1989

Moore, Alan. 'Fossil Angels'. 2010. http://glycon.livejournal.com/13888.html, http://glycon.livejournal.com/14307.html (accessed 16 July 2014)

Narby, Jeremy, and Francis Huxley (eds). *Shamans Through Time: 500 Years on the Path to Knowledge.* London: Thames & Hudson, 2001

Partridge, Christopher. *The Re-Enchantment of the West: Volume 1. Alternative Spiritualities, Sacralization, Popular Culture and Occulture.* London and New York: T&T Clark, 2005

Pollack, Rachel. *Seventy-Eight Degrees of Wisdom.* London: Thorsons, 1980

Vayne, Julian. 'Two Worlds and In-between: The changing concepts of space in modern magick'. In *Magick Works: Stories of Occultism in Theory and Practice.* Oxford: Mandrake of Oxford, 2008

—. 'The Bright Darkness: the entheogenic use of ketamine'. In J. Harold Ellen (ed.), *Seeking the Sacred with Psychoactive Substances: Chemical Paths to Spirituality and to God.* Westport, CT: Praeger, 2014

Wallis, Robert J. 'Between the Worlds: Autoarchaeology and Neo-Shamans'. In Jenny Blain, Douglas Ezzy and Graham Harvey (eds), *Researching Paganisms.* New York: Altamira Press, 2004

Clifton, Chas (ed.). Pomegranate: The International Journal of Pagan Studies. Sheffield: Equinox Publishing. http://www.equinoxpub.com/journals/index.php/POM/index

Hale, Amy, and Dave Green (eds). Journal for the Academic Study of Magic. Oxford: Mandrake of Oxford. http://mandrake.uk.net/journal-for-the-academic-study-of-magic/

From the Vasty Deep:
The reality of DMT entities and other spirits

An essay that attempts to go beyond the simplistic and unhelpful real/not real debate about spirits. First published at theblogofbaphomet.com

The question of the 'reality' or otherwise of aliens/elves/spirit beings seems to be a perennial one. Two recent lectures, at The Birmingham Psychedelic Society and at the Nova Stella pagan moot in London, this was a subject of discussion. Aficionados of N,N-DMT, ayahuasca and some other psychedelics, notably high doses of psilocybin, also get to wrestle with this problem. What are the 'spirits' that we may encounter when in these altered states?

Perhaps one of the greatest modern commentators on the Western encounter with the entheogenic spirit realm is Terence McKenna. He famously and carefully engineered our appreciation of the entities from DMT space. He developed a highly open-ended mythology that permitted multiple interpretations of his nevertheless emphatically held ideas; the importance of psychedelics in the evolution of humans, the existence of intelligence in the DMT experience, and of a world heading towards an apocalyptic omega point. McKenna remains, in much of his writing and lectures, radically uncertain—or perhaps unwilling—to advance a simple single answer to the question 'what are these DMT spirits *really*?'.

Earlier, in the 20th century, Aleister Crowley also addressed the question of the 'reality' of entities such as gods, angels, spirits and demons. He counsels the student of magic to be simultaneously respectful of the phenomena and suspicious of its ultimate origin and meaning. And while Crowley, like McKenna, got swept up within a personal apocalyptic narrative (in Crowley's case that of being The Beast 666), much of AC's work espouses a significant degree of indeterminacy when it comes to the 'reality' of the stories we tell ourselves.

Crowley writes in *Magick in Theory and Practice*:

In this book it is spoken of the Sephiroth and the Paths; of Spirits and Conjurations; of Gods, Spheres, Planes, and many other things which may or may not exist. It is immaterial whether these exist or not. By doing certain things certain results will follow; students are most earnestly warned against attributing objective reality or philosophic validity to any of them.

Psychedelic countercultural hero and outlaw chemist Casey Hardison, in conversation with leading historian of psychedelics Andy Roberts, considers this issue too. In an interview for Robert's book *Acid Drops*, Casey is asked for his views on the objective reality of these entities. In a characteristically brilliant answer Hardison opines thus:

Andy Roberts: *Some people have claimed that during a psychedelic experience they have had contact with/been contacted by what might be termed intelligences or entities. Have you had any such experiences? If so can you give an example?*
Casey Hardison: *I have no certainty this has ever happened to me. I have, however, made shit up to this effect. I tend to think that the molecules themselves are entities. And, they have given me great insight into the vastness of my intelligence. Sure, I've seen the typical machine elves laughing at me and thought ayahuasca was an alien being that resides in my brainstem but I was high at the time.*
AR: *Do you think these experiences represent objective/real experiences involving entities external to the mind/body, whether their origin is earthly, extra-terrestrial, inter-dimensional, aspects of our mind/psyche or a mixture of any of these and more?*
CH: *No. I think that these experiences are personifications of the DNA instincts innate to us. They appear to be generated and sensed by our own brains. Jung would call*

them manifestations of the archetypes. Plato had his perfect forms. I tend to keep it simple and not tool off about possible alien intelligences. In short, I do not know. If there are aliens, I can't wait to try their drugs.

DMT and related tryptamines may flick a neurochemical switch in our heads that induces a sense of 'the real', but that is not the same as saying that the subjective experiences generated by this medicine are real in the same way that these words or your mother are real. While many DMT visions may contain similar content, and while psychedelic drugs may promote conditions where phenomena such as apparent telepathy take place (leading to shared visionary experience), the notion that these chemicals allow us to interface with a 'separate reality', as Castaneda might have put it, is sparse.

Such notions of an 'astral plane' existing as an 'objective' realm in the way our apparent world does are not only the preserve of popular shamanism. Neurologist Andrew Gallimore hopes that one day we can get the dose and duration of DMT right so that; "we can envisage a time in the near future when a brave voyager might spend hours in their [the DMT elves] realm, asking specific questions, performing experiments, and bringing us closer to an independently verifiable relationship with citizens of an alternate universe".

The curious thing (for magicians) is that DMT entities are hailed as 'real' denizens of some imagined—but in no way objectively supportable—alternate universe, whereas gods, ghosts, servitors, nature spirits and all the rest get (perhaps conveniently) forgotten. This perhaps says more about researchers' lack of knowledge about other 'entities' not encountered through mind-bending psychedelics, and their habitual use of real/not real dichotomous conceptual models to understand imaginal entities, than it does about the entities themselves. Sure, when we have our ontological noses tweaked while high on drugs by the dance of a 'jewelled, self-transforming basketball' such as described by McKenna, we may be shocked by what we encounter. However, when people report spirits in other contexts (such as hauntings, channellings, UFO abductions and evocations) many folk are prone to dismiss these as purely subjective perceptions. The unspoken assumption seems to run; 'seeing ghosts=temporal lobe epilepsy or delusional thinking', whereas 'seeing technicolour morphing faces after smoking a crack pipe of DMT=possible evidence of another parallel universe'.

Aside of Gallimore's proposal of getting super high on intravenous DMT, there are other approaches we can try to explore the ontological reality of spirits. One of the best documented examples of this process is the so-called 'Philip Experiment' conducted by the Toronto Society for Psychical Research in the early 1970s. To cut a long and fascinating story short, the group created a fictional entity ('Philip') who they proceeded to 'contact' by deploying the usual technology of spiritualist séances. As one might predict, even though the spirit was 'imaginary', including a backstory that deliberately contained logically contradictory information, the team soon end up getting 'actual' psychic phenomena. Their imagined spirit became 'real.'

How might we, as magicians, as people that work with spirits—with or without the administration of strange drugs—make sense of what's going on and escape the cul-de-sac of Cartesian dualism that demands spirits be either 'real' (in the way that ravens and writing desks are real) or imaginary (by which we really mean 'not real')?

When we begin to unpack the ideas contained in words like 'spirits', we can get closer to a more nuanced appreciation of what may be really going on. 'Spirit' is a small word with a vast collection of potential meanings. Wikipedia observes:

> *The word spirit is often used metaphysically to refer to the consciousness or personality. The notions of a person's spirit and soul often also overlap, as both contrast with body and both are believed to survive bodily death in some religions, and "spirit" can also have the sense of "ghost", i.e. a manifestation of the spirit of a deceased person.*

Let's take the 'spirit' of a human person as our exemplar. Where does that spirit live? What creates it? Out of what stuff does it emerge? Where does it go when the person dies?

Let's start with the body. This is particularly relevant since the word 'spirit' is from the Latin *spiritus* meaning 'breath'. The physical body of a person exists in intimate relationship with the environment. People are born, nourished and raised. As we develop physically, we are admitted into the collective conspiracy of language and culture. Our minds emerge through this network of relationships. The physical architecture of the body itself is also about relationships, it is a vast interplay of electrochemical interactions. If we say that there is a 'spirit' here, that spirit consists of the sum total of these socio-cultural and electrochemical processes. We might say that the spirit is that which we recognise as the holistic entity (the personality) that arises from this complex web of interactions. When it comes to people, we imagine that the spirit dwells somehow within the physical anatomy of the person we associate with it (and in modern Western culture we locate it more specifically in the brain), but in the event of illness or death that spirit may be released from the confines of the body.

For example; it may have been the case that at least one person in ancient Israel was the human individual that inspired the Gospels to be written. If that person lived, they had a body made of interacting physical forces, existing within a cultural space. After death (especially when empowered by the miraculous story of a resurrection) they inhabit instead only the cultural space. This post-mortem entity grows and becomes branded as the 'Spirit of Christ'.

Once we understand that 'spirit' is the word we give to personality or entity that emerges from a series of processes (physical and cultural) we can see why we apply the word in so many contexts. We can meaningfully talk about the spirit of a place, an epoch, an ancestor and more. Does this mean the spirits are 'real'? The answer is clearly 'yes'.

We often encounter this approach in magic where the practitioner is encouraged to embrace their perception of these spirits as 'real' entities. As magician and author Ramsey Dukes and many others have pointed out, imagining that the recalcitrant office photocopier has a personality (as does your car, boat, computer or whatever) confers a variety of advantages as a strategy to interact with such machines. This is hardly surprising because interacting with self-aware entities is what the human nervous system is designed to do. Our brain has evolved to recognise faces above all else, and our whole organism is geared up to interact with other humans. We are a deeply social species. In ceremony when we invoke the gods, we interact with them as though they are 'real' independent beings because that viewpoint provides the best results and it's what we do best.

However, there are other times when we may be only interested in one small set of interactions within a system. By way of an example; if I were a doctor helping a patient with diabetes, while I would want to talk to them as a thinking, feeling, intelligent entity, I would also want to approach the measurement of the level of insulin in the blood as a predominantly mechanical chemical process. It's about using the most appropriate conceptual tool for the job in hand. To give another example with a slightly different emphasis; if I look at a painting, I might describe the image in terms of its location within the canon of Western art (the art historical view). I may decide to talk about the image in terms of what it means to me and how it makes me feel (the personal aesthetic view). If I'm a conservator of paintings I may be primarily interested in the chemical composition of the paints (a purposeful, reductionist mechanical view). Like the wise men feeling the body of the elephant, each view is 'a truth', a 'reality'. Truth is inevitably partial. Depending on what we want to achieve the person, and especially the magician, selects the approach that is the most helpful. Inside the ritual we interact with 'the gods'; outside we may choose to view them as psychological constructs or convenient fictions.

The dichotomy of real/unreal is dissolved by this way of thinking. Breaking down this dichotomy allows us to admit the reality of subjective perception (of ghosts or DMT elves) but doesn't seek blunt Occam's razor and postulate a different order of reality populated by entities that exist in some vaguely hypothesised alternative universe.

A close look at all disincarnate entities, from Father Christmas through to Aeonic Word transmitting Holy

Guardian Angels, shows how these things emerge from within the cultural experience of the person experiencing them. In the case of the haunting of Philip this imagined being was conjured into a certain setting (1970s spiritualism and parapsychology) and true to form behaves in ways that make sense in that context.

In summary we can suggest:

* A spirit is our perception and recognition of an apparently external (i.e. non-self) entity.
* This spirit emerges from a complex set of interactions which may include physical processes (e.g. the spirit of a living person that dwells in their body) and/or cultural forms (e.g. a character in fiction).
* We can choose to interact with the spirit as a separate entity without assuming that it has any kind of 'objective' reality.
* We can choose to interact with one or more of the processes that appear as a spirit entity, and disregard the idea of its apparent personality.
* We can admit the real subjective experience ('I met a ghost') and simultaneously recognise that cultural and other factors inform our experience (in Medieval Europe people met tricksy fairies, in modern America they encounter anal-probing aliens).

During my first journey with ayahuasca I encountered the spirit of the brew as the Queen of the Forest. While I danced and sang in the ceremony a giant mantis-like entity descended from the ceiling and, amusingly, in a voice that sounded rather like British comic Kenneth Williams, said; 'well, how nice to see you here!' Now it may be the case that in some imagined spiritual-quantum-woo alternate universe this being had a radically separate existence and had contacted me from a parallel dimension. I would suggest that the spirit was the emergent property of *Banisteriopsis caapi* + *Psychotria viridis* + the ceremony (which was Santo Daime style, and therefore included songs about the Queen of the

Forest) + my mind (my memories and associations both personal and collective).

This isn't the same as saying the spirit wasn't 'real', for it was undoubtedly a genuine experience for me of an objective entity. Rather, I suggest that the 'spirit' is the sum total of these interactions (including presumably my familiarity with the genius of the camp-Cockney comic) expressed in my awareness, at that time, as an apparently externally manifesting independent, talking entity.

Remember, as Casey says, 'I tend to think that the molecules themselves are entities' which is another statement of this magical approach. DMT entities are real but they live not in a different dimension but instead emerge when human brains meet this molecule. For me this is a much more satisfying answer than anything possible within the dichotomy of real/not real.

This approach to entities places magic and the spirit realm radically within the universe we inhabit, and in my opinion accords much more closely with many animist and panpsychic views of reality both ancient and modern. This approach explains the confusion that ethnographers often face when interacting with animist cultures whether they are researching in 'traditional tribal' or 'modern (post) industrial' contexts; that there often seems to be no hard and fast distinction between people, animals, so-called inanimate objects, 'subjective' feelings, spirit beings, ancestors and gods. While the Cartesian tradition in Western thought desires neat distinctions this isn't how many, or perhaps even most, cultures actually work.

We should, as Dr Gallimore suggests, continue to explore the DMT realm, but I wonder if framing this exploration in terms of a quest to discern whether the elves are 'real' or not, is a profound misunderstanding of the phenomenology of spirits. Or, as The Queen of the Forest in her incarnation as Kenneth Williams might say: 'Stop messing about!'

Baphomet of the Geosphere

Mindfulness in the Museum

A paper written for an academic collection aimed at museum practitioners.

S itting still is a commonplace activity in a museum. We may be resting after a period of exploration, or we may need to take the time to stop and stare; taking in an amazing artwork or historic artefact. We might also be taking the opportunity to 'be-here-now'; using the gallery space as one within which we can practise an increasingly popular technique usually described as 'mindfulness meditation'.

What is Mindfulness?

Since the late 1970s mindfulness, a type of meditation, derived from Buddhist approach of Ānāpānasati (literally 'mindfulness of breathing') has been used in a medical context. The most well-known proponent of this technique is Jon Kabat-Zinn, Professor of Medicine Emeritus and creator of the Stress Reduction Clinic and the Center for Mindfulness in Medicine, Healthcare, and Society at the University of Massachusetts Medical School in the USA. Kabat-Zinn worked to help find techniques that people could use to reduce symptoms of physical pain. Inspired by his own appreciation of Buddhist teachers such as Thich Nhat Hanh and Zen Master Seung Sahn. Zinn introduced meditative techniques into clinical environments and soon found that they had repeatable and scientifically quantifiable benefits for people with chronic pain, including forms of pain that were unresponsive to pharmacological treatments.

In 1991 Zinn published his work in the popular book *Full Catastrophe Living: Using the Wisdom of Your Body and Mind to Face Stress, Pain, and Illness.* By this point he had evidenced the benefits of mindfulness for patients and formalised his approach as Mindfulness Based Cognitive Therapy (MBCT). This approach to mindfulness meditation, although first described in a Buddhist context, was shorn of any explicitly religious or ideological context. This was a technique which could be used to help manage pain ('suffering' as the Buddhists might put it) and could be easily understood as a secular psychological technique. Over the 1990s and into the new millennium the clinical value of mindfulness meditation was subjected to unprecedented scientific scrutiny. It turned out that the benefits of mindfulness did not by any means stop at pain reduction. Study after study demonstrated repeatable effects at both a neurological level via brain imaging studies, as well as cognitive and medical benefits. Some 52 papers were published on the subject of mindfulness based therapies in 2003, rising to 477 by 2012. Nearly 100 randomized controlled trials examining mindfulness had been published by early 2014.

Mindfulness, it is now acknowledged, can help people manage a range of psychological or mental illnesses and other challenges. This includes anxiety and depression. The mindfulness method was formalised by the psychotherapeutic community into the approach known as Mindfulness Based Cognitive Therapy (MBCT). Having an effective, drug-free and therefore relatively inexpensive method of treating these conditions, the focus of more recent research has moved towards exploring the benefits of mindfulness for people who are not 'unwell'. As well as improved sleeping and rest, increased cognitive function and promoting greater psychological resilience, users of mindfulness also reported that they (at least sometimes) actively enjoyed the practice. Perhaps unsurprisingly the opportunity to sit and reflect in a way that privileges the moment, rather than focusing on the past or future, allows people to feel more alive, both during sessions of practice and more broadly in their daily lives.

So what precisely is this new panacea? How does one do mindfulness and, beyond the point made at the start of this essay that mindfulness is traditionally done when sitting still, what does it have to do with museums?

The Body Scan

There are two practices that best exemplify the mindfulness techniques used by contemporary practitioners. The first is called 'the Body Scan'.

The practice is usually performed seated, though in some circumstances it may prove necessary to do the body scan while lying down in bed.

Eyes may be open, down-cast or closed. The feet are flat on the floor if the practitioner is seated on a chair, hands resting on the knees or in the lap. The back is straight but not tense, head resting easily on the neck. It is often recommended that the chin is slightly tucked in. The aim of the posture is to allow the practitioner to sit, reasonably comfortably and still, for the duration of the practice period, usually a minimum of 20 minutes.

At first the practitioner directs their attention to the sensations of sitting in a chair in a particular location and at a particular time. Breathing is normal and there is no deliberate attempt to change respiration (although this will tend to slow and relax as the session progresses). After first paying attention to the whole body the practitioner then begins a mental journey round each part of their body, focusing their attention on one part, then the next, then the next. This movement of attention may be facilitated by the use of words spoken by a therapist or guide; instructions may come from a recording or be issued internally by the practitioner themselves.

Awareness is first brought to, for instance, the toes of the left food. The aim is to simply sense what, if anything arises from this part of the body, in that moment. Critically no attempt to judge or alter the sensations is made. If there is pain or discomfort the aim is that the practitioner simply notices this, allowing the feelings to exist in their own terms without becoming caught up in internal dialogues about how bad/good/worrying or whatever the sensation may be.

The attention is then moved to the top of the foot, the arch, the heel, the ankle and so on. During the practice some people like to imagine their breath flowing into the part of the body they are 'listening to' to help them focus their attention successfully.

After the attention reaches the left hip the process begins again with the toes of the right foot. Once attention has been directed to each part of the right leg it is then brought into the centre of the body. Rising up from the sitting bones, the pelvis and genital area, the back, stomach, and the chest— awareness is brought to bear on each part of the trunk. Once the shoulders are reached, awareness is then shifted to the fingers of the left hand. The attention continues to travel up the left arm, and then the right hand and arm are scanned by the practitioner. At all times the aim is to simply 'sit with' the sensations—or lack of them—that arise from each part of the body. The breath is used as an anchor, along with the voice of the guide or recording, to keep focused on the task.

Once the arms are completed the scan moves on to the neck, throat, face, scalp and even hair. Finally, there is often an opportunity to go back to any particular parts of the body where the practitioner noticed an interesting sensation. Time is given to bring awareness once more to the whole body and the practice ends. It is standard practice to mark the ending and beginning of the session by ringing a singing bowl or bell. There are many variations of this process but the essence of the technique, to pay non-judgemental attention to the actual sensations of the body arising into awareness in each moment, remains constant.

The purpose of the Body Scan is to give the practitioner an opportunity to consciously connect with what's happening for them at a somatic level. People often go through their day with the body as little more than a 'vehicle' from the mind to be carried around in. During this practice it's possible to slow down and allow our bodies to 'speak' to us. Often such 'speaking' only happens when we are in pain but even if during the body scan one experiences pain (for example at the site of an injury) the aspiration is that the pain can be felt in its own terms. Much of the distress that we experience when we are in pain, as Kabat-Zinn discovered, is actually our anxiety about our pain. Practising meeting pain as it arises in the moment can reduce reported levels of pain both during and after the Bond Scan. The practice may also increase feelings of optimism and agency, leading to a much better quality of life.

Meditating in Museums

Over the last four years, sometimes alongside mental health practitioners skilled in mindfulness, I have been teaching the body scan as part of series of drop-in workshops called 'Mindfulness in the Museum'. These sessions have been held at various museums in South West England. The opportunities to explore these techniques in these cultural settings grew out of a major project that I directed in 2010. This project built strong working relationships between cultural sector organisations (museums, coast and countryside services, record office & theatres) and wellbeing support services (mental health services and children's centres) in order to create a vibrant and accessible culture of informal adult learning. A varied programme of activities including metal detecting, family history and a community choir was specifically targeted at people with mental health issues, aiming to increase confidence and reduce isolation. Mental health awareness training was also provided to partner organisations.

Mindfulness at the Museum grew out of this project and has since attracted further funding. The program usually starts in the winter or early spring and generally runs once per week for a set period (typically 8 to 10 weeks). Sessions are held after-hours with participants being invited to the museum for a meeting that last for about one hour.

The format for each session remains consistent each week. After housekeeping is done and introductions are made a short preamble is given about the development of mindfulness meditation. The clinical material and roots of the technique outlined above are briefly described, along with the fact that, outside of the Buddhist spiritual traditions, practices that are akin to mindfulness can be found in Islam (muraqaba), Christianity (contemplative or centring prayer), Taoism (Guan or insight meditation), in ancient humanist beliefs such as those held by various classical philosophies and more modern secular contexts e.g. Open Source Meditation. This preamble helps make each session self-contained. It introduces the techniques so that each meeting is stand-alone allowing sessions to be accessed on a drop-in basis.

Mindfulness happens in the museum and, even where a dedicated education space is available, I deliberately choose to run the session in a gallery space instead. The reason for this is that the atmosphere of the museum is, in my view, directly supportive of the project of mindfulness meditation.

The word 'museum'; itself is of course derived from the Ancient Greek word μουσεῖον (*mouseion*), indicating a place dedicated to the patron divinities of the arts; these buildings are quite literally 'shrines to the Muses'. Within an increasingly secular culture, museums, our shrines to the Muses, are more important than ever. In these places people can be encouraged to draw, or to take photographs (both of which activities encourage better observation), and to sit in contemplation of ourselves and our relationships with others as described through curated spaces. These are multi-denominational temples which exist in many towns, cities and even villages, and they generally aim to be accessible to everyone. They are secular, humanist and inclusive sacred spaces.

Mindfulness of Breath

The quintessential mindfulness technique, which we teach in our programme in addition to the Body Scan, is Mindfulness of Breath or simply Mindfulness Meditation. In this method the practitioner adopts the same posture as in the Body Scan. During the period of sitting the practitioner is asked to focus the attention on their breathing. We expect to find, within a few breaths, other thoughts arising in the mind. These may be memories of the past, perceptions or sensations in the present (such as hearing the sound of traffic outside), hopes or plans for the future. This process of thoughts arising is perfectly normal but, for the duration of the practice, the practitioner chooses to acknowledge these thoughts, and the internal process, then return their attention again to the breath. This cycle continues until the practice ends.

During this practice the person leading the session may say a few words to remind those sitting to interrupt any internal dialogue and return to an awareness of the breath. Critically, the arising of thoughts is an expected process, since the practice in itself is this relationship between being 'mindful' of one thing (the breath), noticing that the mind has shifted its focus (thoughts arising), and returning to the breath. Some practitioners like to label the subject of their thoughts once they become conscious that their attention has moved away from the breath (e.g. 'thinking about what I have to do at work tomorrow'). This seems to help with achieving an objective stance towards the thought, rather than becoming entangled in the associations it could bring. Again, the aim is not to 'stop thinking' or even to become fixed on the idea that one should pay attention only to the breath for 20 minutes (or whatever the duration of the session). This is one of the most important aspects of mindfulness; that there is only the practice. While we may hope for benefits from what we do (improved mental health, relaxation and so on) it is the doing of mindfulness—paying attention to how our minds work—that is the heart of the matter. There is no need to strive for a cessation of mental activity, but only a curiosity to know if this practice of 'sitting with' our thoughts may be interesting and helpful, and a willingness to give this method a try.

While breath is often used as 'an anchor', because it is always available, other anchors for attention in the present moment may be used. This could include doing the washing-up, walking, or contemplation of an object in a gallery. The aim again is to spend time being with the selected sensation in the present moment, and when other thoughts emerge to gently, and compassionately, guide the attention back to the selected anchor for the duration of the practice.

Who teaches Mindfulness?

Mindfulness training courses and resources are now readily available and, while the technique in itself may be straightforward, in order to teach it successfully it is necessary to have practised it assiduously for some time. The reason for this is that various mental states and experiences may be encountered during mindfulness that some people may find confusing, even disturbing. Although the prospect of sitting still and being aware of one's breath for 20 minutes may not sound like an arduous practice, for someone in the throes of mental illness (which statistically affects one in four people in Britain at some point during their lifetime) it can be quite challenging. Being able to manage the problems that people may encounter with mindfulness techniques is an important skill and while training courses are valuable there is no substitute for the experiential learning provided by the direct personal experience of using mindfulness oneself.

Well-being and the Museum

The benefit of mindfulness is that it is simple and approachable, once the technique has been understood all that remains is to apply it and support those who are engaging with it in the museum—or other—context.

As well as its individual benefits, mindfulness also has a social significance since, as it affects us, this inevitably changes our relationships with others. As my colleague Steve Dee expresses it:

> *If Mindfulness practice allows us to slow down and to become more aware of our preconceptions and judgements, it is highly likely that it will allow us to engage with art, history and culture with a new pair of eyes. Greater awareness far from leading to a preoccupation with altered states of consciousness, can lead us in adopting the "beginner's Mind" of the Zen tradition.*
>
> *Our enthusiasm for bringing Mindfulness into public and cultural spaces was based firstly on a desire to emphasise its psychological value detached from religious tradition, and secondly we wanted to provide a means for museums and galleries to recapture their identity as places of spirit.*
>
> *Arguably, many of the challenges to wellness faced by our culture have their roots in isolation, cultural poverty and a sense of historical dislocation. At the risk of sounding*

grandiose, museums, galleries and other cultural spaces have a vital role in addressing these needs. Whether via an art show or a display about wartime gardening, our role is not to tell people what to think, rather it is to act as a catalyst to curiosity and reflection.

For people wanting to explore mindfulness the only requirement is curiosity; the curiosity to wonder whether these techniques could help them. This 'help' may be framed in terms of addressing illness or dis-ease, but it may also be imagined as a technique that can help us explore and improve our lives in a more general sense. This curiosity is the central human drive that museums seek to tap into when they present the wonderful things held in their collections. Evoking this curiosity about who we are, in these spaces, using these techniques, seems to me to provide some unique opportunities.

Baphomet mask, made by Erisian Garbs, on loan to The Museum of Witchcraft & Magic, Boscastle, Cornwall from The British Isles Section of The Magical Pact of The Illuminates of Thanateros

Stoned Temple Pilots:
Set, Setting and Substance in Contemporary Entheogenic Spirituality

A lecture delivered at the mother of all psychedelics conferences Breaking Convention at the University of Greenwich, London in 2013 and reproduced in their publication Neurotransmissions: Psychedelic Essays from Breaking Convention.

I want to speak today about a community of practitioners who are variously named and exist in Britain, throughout Europe and in many other lands. They are shamans, magicians, witches and followers of what we might call the 'medicine path'. These are a courageous group of people who are attempting to deploy an archaic method of spiritual enquiry that, in some cases, our culture currently legislates against in the strongest terms.

A recent case comes to mind:

In September to November of 2010, seven members of the Santo Daime church in the UK were arrested and placed on bail. Containers of Santo Daime (ayahuasca) were seized and shown to contain DMT and a police investigation was launched. At this time charges were brought only against one person while the other six people remained on bail. The charge was Fraudulently Evading Prohibition on a Banned Substance. In these initial stages of the case the defence legal team gathered evidence and expert witness statements to show the legal ambiguity of the status of ayahuasca, as well as the bona fide nature of Santo Daime as a religious practice, the proven health benefits of this medicine, and lack of proof of harm concerning the sacrament. All this information was put before the Director of Public Prosecutions (DPP) who then agreed to conduct a review of the case. The results of this review were that five people were released from bail without any further charges, but the DPP decided to pursue prosecutions against two individuals. In addition to the previous charges they were also charged with conspiracy to import a banned substance.

There are many plants and chemicals being deployed by groups that are not prohibited in the nations within which they are being used. But where a violation of local law does occur the penalties can be severe. In the case of the two Santo Daime members charged in this case they remained on bail for over two years. I am however pleased to say that, following magical work, spells and prayers that were deployed by many of the 'medicine community' (as I shall describe these practitioners) the State has chosen to 'drop the case' for reasons of insufficient evidence. The fact that tens of litres of ayahuasca is deemed 'insufficient evidence' is clear proof of the power of magick.

Stealthopolis drops the beat; and the case against members of the Santo Daime Church.

I've been fortunate to encounter and, at times, share ceremonial space, with a variety of people within this 'medicine community'.

I have no idea how widespread these communities are. Considerations of security and probity are paramount, so I have little notion of the scale of these networks. My sense is that there are perhaps thousands of medicine practitioners in the British Isles. This ranges from solitary practitioners who might identify as 'traditional witches' and who make use of herbs such as datura and mandrake, through to much more organised, communal religions such as the Santo Daime church.

Having set the scene and explained the limits of my knowledge I'd like to describe a few rituals. These are not by any means cases studies but are best understood as phenotypic examples—composed of elements from different sources in order to create a composite of a ceremony's observable characteristics. They are entheogenic ritual mash-ups if you will.

The first ceremony takes place in a little village in Britain. The two participants call themselves witches, one man, one woman. The man has spent days brewing ayahuasca in his kitchen. He has chanted in his own language as he made the brew. Singing the famous icaro of Terrence McKenna 'row, row, row your boat, gently down the stream...' while stirring the mixture. The plants; the vine and leaves, have been obtained from an online herbal supplier. He jokingly calls this 'boil in the bag' ayahuasca. The male witch is familiar with ayahuasca having taken it in his visits to South America. The female witch has never taken the potion before; she plans to use this as an opportunity to enter the spirit world through a new doorway (she has an intensely animist view of the universe). The man wants to use this medicine to help heal the cancer of a family member.

Together they cast a circle in a Wiccan style. They call on the spirits of the four directions to protect them and inspire them. They both drink, and for the next two hours they sit. The woman is silent and motionless throughout, the man shakes a rattle, a constant beat—tsk, tsk, tsk, tsk, tsk... until the rite is done.

The male witch, when he finds himself in the right part of the vision, sees the cancer cells inside the body of the person he's seeking to heal. Strange spirit forms appear that look like aircraft, vaguely reminiscent of Steampunk Wellington bombers, travelling through the body of the patient. They train their guns on the diseased cells and blast them with rays of electricity.

The female witch's journey remains her own. It is regarded as good practice to keep one's personal experiences and insights to oneself after ceremony, as describing them can alter their import, or intrude upon other's process when sitting as a group.

At the end of the ceremony, the participants thank the spirit of the medicine from the land of the great river. They go outside to breathe in the night air, to touch the bare earth and let their intentions go into the world.

(As a supplement to this account, and to help you develop the charming meta belief that magick works, I'd like to add that the cancer in question was successfully cured.)

Another ceremony. This time in a tepee, based on the peyote ritual of the Native American Church. There is a Grandfather peyote button on the crescent moon altar at the centre of the space, but the medicine is psilocybin mushrooms preserved in honey. As with the previous ceremony there is the same rapid rhythm, this time produced by a traditional water drum. The staff and rattle move round the circle, pulling the drum behind them, every person who wants to has a chance to sing.

Long-time members of the group know the Native American chants and sing out Others know English language Pagan chants, and these are shared in the circle too. At significant points throughout the ceremony, handfuls of cedar incense is used to cleanse the space and tobacco is smoked as prayers are offered. There is the Midnight Water, which provides a chance to stand up, leave the tepee and urinate as well as to have some water to drink, and in the morning breakfast (deer meat, fruit and corn) serves to confirm that this is very much the peyote circle 'design' (a word these practitioners rather like).

During the ritual the ceremonial 'arrow fire' is swept into astonishing patterns; a heart is formed from the raked out glowing coals, then a great fiery bird. At one point the fire is separated into two and then brought back together again.

The leader of the ceremony explains the core technique behind this complex ceremonial event to me:

'Especially when we are using peyote', he says, *'the approach of our ceremony is quite different from psychoanalysis. Rather than dredging up our problems and trying to work on them we instead fill ourselves with joy. We fill ourselves with gratitude; we look to be conscious of the many, many ways in which we are blessed. In this way we push out the sadness, drive it away and open ourselves to the blessing of the Great Spirit.'*

This kind of neo-tribal ritual is of course enacted in the much larger—though in many ways as deeply codified—ritual, of the free party or rave.

In a city in the south west of England a warehouse has been overrun by outlaws. Inside the space, balanced on old trucks, is a vast sound system. The dark space is punctuated by fluorescent lights and UV glows. The deep drum pounds the rhythm, the heartbeat of the city; duf, duf, duf, duf, duf.

In a canopied chillout area there are banners of Shiva Nataraja and images of the trumps from the tarot of Freda Harris and early entheogenic enthusiast Aleister Crowley. Here people are kissing, receiving massages, smoking and talking.

Cannabis and MDMA are the primary medicines in evidence, and while this may not be conceptualised by the majority as some form of spiritual practice the 'design' of the ceremony, its gnostic technology, is clearly analogous to that of the peyote circle ceremony: driving out the sadness with joy, with ecstasy.

Allow me to tell another couple of stories.

The first is of a ceremony in which ketamine is the sacrament. In this ritual a huge projection screen has been erected in a warehouse space, but this time the people at the party are by invitation only. On the screen a film is about to be shown, a computer simulation of the journey through the

Sushumna, the spinal column and axis mundi of Indian esoteric anatomy. The explicit aim of the ceremony is to catalyse a direct experience of the non-dual nature of reality. Participants sit or lounge on the floor which is covered with fluffy blankets, cushions and the occasional cuddly toy—there are furry snakes and soft, friendly, white tigers.

Travelling through each chakra in turn, following the raising journey of the kundalini snake, the film contains beautifully crafted computer graphics. The human body is shown in space, vibrating with coloured lights and other iconography of this mythic journey. The traditional Hindu symbols associated with each mystical centre are depicted; lotuses, Sanskrit letters and deities, as well as fantastic fractal designs in hues corresponding with each region of the subtle anatomy.

Each participant is offered a moderate dose of ketamine, via insufflation, before the film and again halfway through the screening as the serpent arrives at the heart centre. These lines of magical white powder are racked out on a great ceremonial mirror. During the movie the woman leading the ceremony sings the Bīja mantras at appropriate points and describes the attributes of each chakra, there is a background soundtrack of the seed syllable mantra, carrying participants through this experience which lasts approximately one hour. Those experienced psychonauts serving the medicine take only low doses and are on hand to help with any difficulties should they arise (in this instance, none did). From the conversations afterwards, many people had an amazing, beautiful experience.

The next ceremony is one in which participants gather outside in a circle of trees. There is a drum singing, I expect by now you know the rhythm...

There are voices too, calling on the Great Spirit, the life-force of the universe.

Participants process along a spiral path into the centre of the circle, as they do so they are imagining that they are walking across the vast swathes of time since the creation of our world up to the present moment, visualizing the forms of life proliferating upon our planet through the aeons. Once assembled round the edge of the circle they go through a series of yogic stretches. Relaxing and opening their somatic selves for the experience to come.

At the centre of the space they partake of substances representing the four elements; honey for fire, scented herbs for air, water and the smell and touch of soil for earth. On the ground are blankets and animal skins. The centre of the circle is where the participants 'take the trance', each offered a large hit from a pipe containing 5-Meo-DMT. This represents the element of spirit, the self-conscious coming into awareness of the life-force of our planet, the fifth element of this Eucharistic rite. Ritual chanting and drumming continues throughout the ceremony. As people who have smoked the 5-MeO-DMT emerge from the experience they too join in the chorus of voices.

At the end of the ritual, after everyone who journeyed has returned from their trance, the participants thank the spirits of the place; they laugh and hug one another saying "good to see you Brother, good to see you Sister!"

With these archetypal examples in mind what can we say about this 'medicine community'?

The first point is that these rituals represent something active in the zeitgeist.

The notion that drug use might have for some (at a rave) or for all participants (as in the other examples) a spiritual dimension is far from alien these days in our culture. For while discourses about the harm and horror of drugs are commonplace so too is the idea that substances like LSD can fuel personal transformation and be allies in the creative processes of visual art, science, music, philosophy and more. Many people are, through the media, increasingly aware of both ancient and modern cultures in which the use of sacred medicines is normal and accepted.

We live in a chemical world, and so the notion of spiritual experience as being something which might be augmented or generated by chemicals is quite intelligible. This view of spirituality is very new and quite different from much of the

Western cultural tradition. It is perhaps easy to see it as an expression of a presumed archaic sensibility; namely that all things are connected, and that matter and spirit are not separate things. But whether this is a new or old idea really doesn't matter, the bottom line is that by permitting the possibility of psychedelics having a role in spirituality, religion makes sense not just for 'tribal people' but for us in the modern post-industrialised world here and now. Moreover, there are now several generations of people in Britain who have grown up during the time of the psychedelic underground. Their parents (or even grandparents) took acid back in the day, they themselves did pills and danced until dawn, and they are aware that when their kids get older, they may be meeting drugs with long and exotic chemical names. Despite the threatening consequences of illegality, the number of people who have accessed the psychedelic state continues to increase, giving rise to 'underground' or 'countercultures' and even family traditions of getting high. It's therefore unremarkable that for some people developing their engagement with these experiences in a spiritual, ceremonial way is something they are inspired to do.

Spirituality is an active attempting to connect with the sacred. The word 'religion' points to much the same thing, though arguably emphasising a more passive approach to this process. Our (re)connection to the sacred can be imagined as a healing process. On the ground this might look like people breaking addictions or entrenched patterns of behaviour, getting more self-actualised, becoming more compassionate, and getting into better relationship with themselves, those around them, and the planet as a whole. If this is healing, then the idea that drugs might help us heal makes total sense.

A second point is that many practitioners of this Western Medicine Way, while having great respect for the native elements of 'designs' such as the peyote ceremony, see their own practices as ongoing, unfolding spiritual systems rather than attempts to ape traditional entheogenic use. When I went to my first Santo Daime ceremony the songs were all in Portuguese, but these days' many songs are in English, and other languages now form part of the repertoire.

British neo-Paganism has grappled with its modern origins, by and large coming to terms with them successfully—acknowledging that it is inspired by, rather than the direct descendant of, pre-Christian religion. This willingness to embrace the unfolding of a new spirituality, rather than feeling the need to legitimise practice as old, authentic and/or native, has created a richly syncretic culture. This is clearly demonstrated by my last two examples which are attempts to create a ritual 'design' that provides a suitable space for the deployment of two human synthesised substances, one of which (ketamine) is a chemical which, as far as we know, has only existed on this planet for half a century. In this way modern medicine communities are certainly shamans in the sense that Mircea Eliade uses the term. They are 'technicians of the sacred', adopting designs, tweaking, augmenting and developing their approaches to generating ecstatic and often healing experiences on the part of themselves and their communities.

Some of the rituals I've mentioned maintain this future orientation not only by virtue of using new entheogens (MDMA and Ketamine) but by creating and managing spaces in which modern technologies may play an important role. This is creating set and setting for the substance using the most appropriate and engaging tools available. The fast flow of information, even in these often clandestine communities, means that songs, methods and ideas move around pretty fast. Cultural drift, syncretism and the garnering of new techniques and tricks happens so quickly and overtly that claims of a style being set in stone simply don't wash any longer.

Another important feature demonstrating the adaptive nature of humans is the fact that these environments being created to 'hold space' are deeply informed by a relationship with the medicine. 'The medicine lets you know what conditions it likes', said one practitioner to me recently. The rave is a large-scale version of this process. The drug, MDMA, comes into Western culture and we create environments designed to maximise its potential. So too in these more explicitly spiritual settings, the psychoactive speaks to those who take it and is an active co-creator of the ceremonial process. But, just like evolution, this doesn't create a single type of entity and there are many responses that may work for a given time, individual or purpose. Careful attention to the setting of drug experience is a deeply ritualising process and those on the medicine path have a cornucopia of methods and traditions to inform them. But the spirit of the medicine speaks, and often in a highly animist way. The people who developed the ketamine ritual design described above contacted the spirit of ketamine, the 'Goddess Ketamina' and her dolphin familiar 'Snorky'. Through repeated visionary explorations with that substance a ritual design was developed suitable for tens of people, keeping the experience sacred, safe and spectacular.

The nature of these groups is in some ways similar to the classical mystery religions or cults of the ancient Greco-Roman world. Secret initiatory processes were conducted under the auspices of a particular deity—Mithras, Kybele, (the Magna Mater), Orpheus, Isis, Dionysus or Demeter, whose cult temple at Eleusis stood for over a thousand years. Each of these ancient cults gave the initiate an opportunity to make a special and personal connection to a particular spirit, which in terms of the ways these things were imagined in the ancient world is probably a more accurate term than 'god'.

This was done through experience, and whether these ancient designs used entheogens is anyone's guess. But here and now in the modern day, the medicine community is certainly an initiate community. There is the act of taking the sacrament in the sacred space and whether you do it once or many times this is a brave initiatory act. There is no safe word once you've taken that pill, or powder, or potion. For this reason, and for being brave enough to explore the development of safe, sane and sacred ways of using these powerful medicines in a climate of great fear and hostility, I salute the members of the modern medicine way.

These are the facts:

* That our culture finds the idea of entheogenic religious experience intelligible.
* That these techniques are fluid—they are rapidly shared, adaptable to contemporary conditions and quickly hybridise,
* That the medicine itself speaks to participants and they enter a dialogue with it.
* That entering this dialogue constitutes a form of initiatory practice.

Given that this is the case, I submit that the entheogenic genii are well and truly out of the bottle. And, that our culture should and indeed must change to accommodate this phenomenon. In practice this means changes first and foremost in drug legislation. I believe that not only should the religious or spiritual use of drugs be permitted, but wider uses, since there are great recreational—as well as clear medical—possibilities contained in these materials.

It's true that a defence of religious or ethnic use cannot alone oppose the current trajectory of drug legislation (the recent banning of Khat in the UK is a good, or rather bad, example of this). However, one should bear in mind that human beings draw much of their personal and social strength from their peak spiritual and religious experiences. And in this sense the use of sacred drugs is an engine for social change.

We know that the 'drug problem' is tied closely to big business, criminal cartels, tremendous human suffering, covert government activity and other unpleasant things. For me tackling this issue raises the possibility of bringing, as the medicine community does, heaven and earth together. If we, as a global community, can work to have a better relationship with these physical materials, which themselves can be the basis of the transcendental experience, perhaps we can perfect what the alchemists of old were attempting. We can take the base metal; the horror of the drug war, and transmute it into the gold of a new spirituality which can serve our planet well as we build the third millennium.

And I pray that the insights, the wisdom the and power of these medicines can one day be a full and beloved part of our culture.

Through the Looking-Glass

Reflections on magic, identity, and cross-dressing.

Ritual is a series of inhabited metaphors. It seeks to make meaning, through the actualisation of desire, and to reflect this meaning back into the wider world. A magick ritual is often the distillation of a long internal process. It is the 'visible manifestation' of a multi-layered narrative of meditation, deep listening, curiosity and intentionality. Such was the ritual I had created for a meeting of magicians in the summer of 2011. This ritual found me dressed as Alice in Wonderland (powder blue dress, petticoat, white and black striped stockings, buckled high heels) in my subterranean temple. A projector flashed images on the ceiling of the chamber, a parade of various interpretations of Carroll's Alice mythos; from the original drawings of John Tenniel to stills from Tim Burton's movie of 2010. The other eight participants were costumed, giggling and (as I'd instructed) behaving playfully. Bubbles filled the air as I began the invocation:

> 'Twas brillig, and the slithy toves
> Did gyre and gimble in the wabe:
> All mimsy were the borogoves,
> And the mome raths outgrabe.

The purpose of the ritual was to consecrate a magical mirror. This looking glass, inscribed with the eight-rayed star of chaos, and bearing the legend 'Nothing is True, Everything is Permitted", would become part of our ceremonial regalia. The design itself has been rendered by a Brother in Aotearoa, The Island of The Long White Cloud (aka New Zealand). The mirror would be one of a pair, one to be located in Britain and one in the New Zealand. We were creating a rabbit hole with this circular looking glass, leading through the earth, to the antipodes and into other realities.

> *Down, down, down. Would the fall never come to an end! 'I wonder how many miles I've fallen by this time?' she said*

aloud. `I must be getting somewhere near the centre of the earth. Let me see: that would be four thousand miles down, I think... Presently she began again. 'I wonder if I shall fall right through the earth! How funny it'll seem to come out among the people that walk with their heads downward! The Antipathies, I think—' (she was rather glad there was no one listening, this time, as it didn't sound at all the right word) '—but I shall have to ask them what the name of the country is, you know. Please, Ma'am, is this New Zealand or Australia?'*

"Magick", as a wise Adept once informed me, "is all about smoke and mirrors".

"Take some more tea," the March Hare said to Alice, *very earnestly.*

Two Sisters held the magical mirror while the rest of the group made their connection to that child-like state of wonder, and dreamlike confusion. "What disorientates you", as Timothy Leary observed, "is good". Poems and rhymes dredged up from our playground memories, memories of spinning around and around and around, manic laughter. A sense of curiosity that is at once playful yet mysteriously foreboding. This is the sense we have in the Alice books, the sense we have when we pass through the looking glass and the sacred substances thereon. Changes in scale, like Alice shrinking and growing, may happen. I'd offered participants in the rite a bottle labelled 'Drink Me' and a sweetmeat on a dish labelled 'Eat Me' as they entered the Temple. These contained nothing more remarkable than water and candied ginger but after a whole day of other ritual work the atmosphere was just what I had hoped for, a blend of gentleness and fun, shot through with streaks of wild mania.

It was all very well to say "Drink me," but the wise little Alice was not going to do that in a hurry: "no, I'll look first," she said "and see whether it's marked 'poison' or not".

A common idea in much contemporary magic, particularly in the chaos style, is that rituals are about creating a certain atmosphere, fully inhabiting that, and using this 'total environment' (as The Temple of Set might describe it) as the theatre of transformation. This approach is a species of sympathetic or memetic magic. This method puts me in mind of 'partner blending' in Aikido. The ritual environment, and all the work that has gone into creating the practice, aims to engender a certain state of mind. By adopting, inhabiting and then transforming that state we open up new possibilities in the world. This is the magician as alchemist; the mind is the prima materia, ritual paraphernalia are the double-pelican flasks, retorts and other devices of alchemy. This is results magick which, whether it works by re-programming our individual psyches which then have a cascading effect in the wider world, or some more mysterious process, certainly works. Magick is first and foremost an individual transformative journey. Our minds are, unsurprisingly, more immediately amenable to change than the conditions which surround us. The Great Work begins at home.

'There is no use trying,' said Alice; 'one can't believe impossible things'.

'I dare say you haven't had much practice,' said the Queen. 'When I was your age, I always did it for half an hour a day. Why, sometimes I've believed as many as six impossible things before breakfast.'

But I'm not the only 'Alice' present. On the altar sits a power object, a memento of a 'cultural descendant'. In a small wooden box there is a stone, a plaster coated fragment from a wall. This was brought back by a dear Brother and Sister from their visit to Cefalù and the site of the former Abbey of Thelema. At my request they obtained a souvenir for me from that place (which I had visited many years before). I'd imagined my gift as perhaps a leaf from the trees that now surround 'the haunted house' as it is known locally, or perhaps some earth from outside the building. But I was gifted something far more impressive. The stone had been found in a room known as The Chamber of Nightmares. This was Crowley's bedroom, temple, drug den and alchemical crucible. I hasten to add that the stone was lying on the floor, where it had fallen loose from the wall. This wall had been painted, and the stone in the box showed signs of black and red and green pigments. The literal marks of The Beast!

Beast in a Box

In the Sicilian sunshine Crowley had gathered his experimental community about him. The Chamber of Nightmares was his lair, a place covered with his naïve art depicting women in agonised erotic forms and famously his doggerel couplet dedicated to the Scarlet Woman:

Stab your demonic smile to my brain
Soak me in cognac, cunt and cocaine.

The Abbey of Thelema was also a place where Crowley got to play dress up. He'd transform himself, with skirts and rouged lips, into 'Alyce' and, according to legend, try to seduce his male students. This ritual transvestism, like most things in magick, was both personal and pan-cultural. Crowley was resolutely bisexual and, as is well known, also had plenty of what today we rather timidly call 'issues'. His magick is very much about rebelling, experimenting and coming to terms with his own sexual nature in a climate of fear and legal oppression. In some respects, he enjoyed confronting the sin-obsessed Victorian culture of his time with outrageous behaviour although, like most great storytellers his tales probably talk-up how outré he could be. But it was the hypocrisy of it all that really enraged Crowley, he writes; "Part of the public horror of sexual irregularity so-called is due to the fact that everyone knows himself essentially guilty."

Like that other founder of a modern Pagan religion Gerald Gardner, Crowley was able to build his kinks into his religion of Thelema. This is not to say these religions are actually elaborate ruses to allow 'dirty old men' to get their kicks. Instead it is the very fact of making sacred our expressions of pleasure, and of realising the capacity of our kinks to induce mystical levels of ecstasy, that demands that we enshrine our deepest desires at the heart of our spirituality. Magick is a technology rooted not in purely theoretical and intellectual worlds but embedded directly in the body. To use our sexual desires to empower us, to help in our process of autopoiesis, is solid tantric doctrine which was rediscovered in the context of modern magic by Crowley and Gardner.

My kink, like Uncle Al's in his Abbey days, is cross-dressing. Cross-dressing is an interesting cross-cultural phenomenon. A brief exploration of cultures, both ancient and modern, suggests that cross-dressing seems to be ubiquitous. Curiously in these days of nuanced psychological theory and neurological exploration there are few good models to explain why this is. But there are the hijra in India, the kathoey of Thailand, the 'two-spirit' people found in most of the nations of Native American culture. There is the curious way that many priests, both Roman-Catholic or Greek-Orthodox for instance, wear robes which, in other settings, may be easily (mis)understood as dresses. There are all those ritual cross-dressing devotees of classical antiquity and the festivals of reversal, such as Saturnalia, where social roles and clothes get mixed up. There are stag parties and rugby club nights out; female to male pirates like Anne Bonny... the list goes on. It would appear that many cultures maintain more complex gender identity structures than that naïvely compartmentalised assumption that men and women come from different planets.

By dressing as Alyce Crowley was in step with other Victorian radicals such as his lover, the art collector and stage female impersonator, Jerome Pollitt. Pioneers like Pollitt and Crowley (for Crowley, whatever your judgement of the man, was certainly a pioneer) were pushing back the social and sexual mores of the time. This is a good example of how the personal connects with the collective. There's no need here for parapsychological spooky occult effects; magick in this sense is the heroic, radical transformation of the self; a transformation that can change the World.

In 1967, a year before I was born and 20 years after Crowley's death, male homosexuality was decriminalised in Britain. While there is no equivalence between cross-dressing and homosexuality or bisexuality, there is a relationship. Cross-dressing, or at any rate 'flamboyant' dress, is part of the notion of the 'effeminate male' and is therefore an aspect of the story of homosexuality. (I'm putting aside here the issue of the construction of ideas such as sexual orientation in itself—interested readers are recommended to explore the work of Michel Foucault). Cross-dressing, while not punished as severely as 'sodomy', does attract a Biblical censure in the book of Deuteronomy (22:5): "A woman must not wear men's clothing, nor a man wear women's clothing, for the Lord your God detests anyone who does this."

In late 20th century Europe and America men—as openly as circumstances permitted—loving men and agitating for the acceptance of their behaviour, overturned millennia of religious, cultural and legal repression. Cross-dressing likewise is an act which, however public one may be about it, has a deeply subversive quality. It challenges the status quo of simplistic dualities, of this and that, by introducing 'the other'. Challenging the repressions within culture through our actions is what makes and transforms culture.

It's easy to get lost in the proliferation of identities, territories and nomenclature when discussing gender and sexuality; my own preferred term is 'queer' and characters like Crowley, in many respects, are profoundly queer. The Queer are the perpetrators of transgressive acts that upset the applecart of cultural norms. They remind us that, while making territory and identity is a natural and important part of the human experience, it's essential that we peer over our self-imposed fences every now and again. That we acknowledge, as cross-dressing does in and of itself, that for every two sides to an issue, there is always the slim but impossible to forget third possibility: the liminal edge between heads and tails, between what we are, and what we are not.

> *"I wonder if I've been changed in the night? Let me think. Was I the same when I got up this morning? I almost think I can remember feeling a little different. But if I'm not the same, the next question is 'Who in the world am I?' Ah, that's the great puzzle!"*

My own cross-dressing started when I was about eight. I recall pulling on a pair of my mother's tights. I'd found them in what we called in our family 'the useful box', this was a chest kept in our spare bedroom which contained all manner of things that could be used for children's craft activities; toilet roll tubes, egg boxes, cardboard, and on this particular day an old pair of tan-coloured pantyhose.

I don't know why I tried them on and this is partly the beauty of cross-dressing. Yes, it may have been some repressed or sublimated urge seeking expression. It may have been some 'warped' form of gender identification, a medically describable 'gender dysphoria'. It may have been the desire to transgress social norms, to wear myself what I understood perfectly well were 'ladies' things'. It may have been a desire to experiment, to know in some way 'what it feels like to a girl'. Perhaps it was the sense of being encased in something, being tightly held, feeling a novel and exotic fabric on my body, a new sensation. Whatever the reason I found myself with them on, and over the years that followed I would take further secret opportunities to cross-dress.

> *I can't explain myself, I'm afraid, Sir, because I'm not myself you see.*

There were times when, as a cognitive psychologist might put it, this behaviour reduced; even though there was still cross-dressing ideation. I was a goth while at college and being a passionate fan of David Bowie, I backcombed my hair and wore impossibly tight trousers. Cuban heeled boots and plenty of make-up was de rigueur for several years. At other periods in my life these activities were less prominent. It's pretty hard to do much about cross-dressing when you're working cutting logs in the cork forests of Spain or digging an allotment in Sussex. But I'd say that my own 'Alice' was always with me. Through forays into kink culture at the famous BDSM club 'Torture Garden', and changes in my relationships, this aspect of me began to emerge more radically from the proverbial broom closet. I discovered the work of Pagan gender theoreticians such as Raven Kaldera, and began a new relationship with a lover who was supportive and indeed appreciative of my newly acquired wardrobe.

In this sense my subterranean ceremony was also for me a species of 'coming out'.

My Sisters holding the mirror were seated on chairs I'd designed for the ritual; carved with wooden heart shapes, painted white, red and black, with criss-crossing chess-board design and decoupage playing cards.

As the ritual progressed, we'd reach the state I was after; a laughing, wild wonder, the kind of blend of fear and delight that attends us when we first experience a firework display.

We pour this energy into the mirror to the strains of Jefferson Airplane's *White Rabbit*, linking the Alice mythos with the acid-fuelled culture that was the dawn of the modern psychedelic revolution.

One pill makes you larger, and one pill makes you small...

Finally, there is a banishing with laughter and we emerge, transformed and blinking from the underground temple and up into the light. We've passed into Wonderland, through the looking glass and into a world that is changed in a curious way. My clothes are appropriately dishevelled and, since this is the last ritual for this meeting, I'm able to spend the rest of the night sitting around on cushions, comfortable in my dress, surrounded by my friends. Full of wonder and free from fear.

Salutations to Him who is free from fear!

The Typology of Magick

First published at theblogofbaphomet.com, a wry look at the stylistic differences between modern schools of esotericism.

I was at a gallery private view recently when a colleague told me that she's been looking me up online. 'I didn't realise you were a chaos magician,' she remarked, 'isn't that quite—dark?'

I'm pretty lucky in that I'm out as a Pagan and occultist at work, and employed within a sector in which religious or philosophical beliefs that don't conflict with our policies about equality of opportunity, anti-racism, and an LGBTQ+ - positive agenda shouldn't be a problem. In fact, in an area such as Devon where over 95% of the population identify as 'white British' and of which the majority describe themselves as 'Christian', my own beliefs perhaps go some way towards to creating a more diverse culture.

In my brief explanation of chaos magic (CM) to my colleague I touched on ideas such as fractals and chaos mathematics, which exhibit self-similarity at different scales, and the analogous observation that different spiritual traditions exhibit similar techniques of praxis even where their exoteric credo may appear very distinct. I mentioned the idea of Khaos in the ancient Greek sense of the term; the unknowable void from which arise the many formed manifestations of the universe.

Santa Maria Chaos

CM can also be described in terms of its historical development, a particular approach or style of spiritual endeavour. One that developed in Europe from a confluence of late 20th century ideas; ceremonial magic, neo-paganism, Discordianism and more. As a style it was influenced by the punk, do-it-yourself ethos; an intensely personal quest to discover magic for ourselves rather than having it filtered through the then dominant theology of Thelema or Wicca.

The use of the term 'chaos' in its modern sense does suggest, as my colleague had surmised, a certain 'darkness'. But what in practice does this mean? One way of understanding this might be to consider CM as having a particular flavour, a style in the sense that there are styles of clothing, of music or martial arts.

As humans there are different trends that appeal more or less to each of us at certain points in our lives. As a younger man I experimented with dressing in punk, Oscar Wilde-esque, goth and other styles of clothing. These days I've added cultural sector professional, Freemason and cross-dresser to the list. While in their practice chaos magicians might draw on different paradigms or expressions of spirituality (or other methods of esoteric investigation) there is, nevertheless, a certain style or flavour to something we designate as 'chaos' magic.

Humans being humans it's pretty common to find some people (mostly those who are rather new to occultism in my experience) asserting the primacy of their own preferred approach. More experienced practitioners tend to realise that, while there are differences in forms of occultism, these are outweighed by their similarities. Even in apparently über-radical/traditionalist styles of magic, when one examines their embodied practice, one finds methods for changing consciousness, magic circles, spooky barbarous words and songs. As they say in the Orient, 'same same but different'.

Another way of thinking about the relationship between esoteric styles is that of music. Music comes in different genres. It consists of sounds—and the absence of sounds—placed into relationships and while it may be challenging to specify exactly what music *is,* we can all recognise the various forms in which it appears (i.e. what it *does*).

As a former graphic designer one of my favourite ways to consider the relationship of different occultures is as styles of lettering. The kind of fonts used on publications aimed at aficionados of a given tradition tells us something about the aspirations and sense of self in that culture or 'market'. It also tells us how that tradition (especially in these days of self-publishing) would like to present itself to the world. Thus the word 'chaos' in the examples below, culled from both print and online esoteric publications, is a bit alien/futurist/goth—this is a youthful font, wild and certainly 'dark'. Then we have 'Druid'; folkish and friendly. 'Shaman' is strong, 'ethnic', suggesting hand carved shapes, delighting in the simplicity of only upper case. 'Thelema' is classic, authoritative; perfect for a religion with a sacred book and reams of texts catalogued into classes A, B, C etc. 'Witch' suggests a wildness (the letters don't sit evenly on the line), a slightly retro feel with those uneven serifs and hand-crafted edges.

Many faced magic

Taking this method of analysis a little deeper we can focus our attention on just one sector of occulture and see how the choice of fonts reflects the various flavours which that style itself contains. Again, these examples are from contemporary esoteric publications.

CHAOS
Druid
SHAMAN
THELEMA
WITCHES

Mysterious writes

The first font (and yes, it is actually called 'Wiccan') again suggests something very much at the human-scale, hand crafted and simple. The moon like 'C's may subtly allude to the nocturnal symbolism of witchcraft. The next reversed-out text is more authoritative but maintains an olde worlde feel (the 'W' and ligature of the 'f' and 't' put one in mind of early modern type). The more elaborate grey text on black goes for that spooky vibe. Based on an imagined late medieval Gothic illuminated lettering, this text has an additional sprinkling of ye olde scroll work. The line 'The quick brown fox' is set in the kind of font one finds in the seminal book *Witches* by Erica Jong and illustrated by Joseph A. Smith. It is cursive, romantic and again with that suggestion of times past when people wrote with pens. The bottom right lettering, originally printed in scarlet, reprises the above observations with an old fashioned hand-written italic font. By taking examples of fonts like this we can discern the stylistic elements that appeal to people who like witchcraft: the medieval and the gothic, and the folkish hand-crafted (as opposed to industrial).

Take a browse round the library, the bookshop or online and one can easily see how the fonts we choose reflect our identity and the spells we hope to cast through writing upon the world.

When people ask me 'what is chaos magic?' especially if they know something about occulture, the letter style analogy is one I often use. What we are all doing, in our different ways is 'magic', the wrapper we choose for our practice, like the selection of typefaces, is about the style we find most evocative and inspirational at any given time as we make our journey into the Mystery.

The Sun is Eclipsed by the Moon

A ritual in honour of a solar eclipse.

I wake late. No time for elaborate costume or other devices. I had thought to do something more complex, to go to the sea and watch the eclipse happen over the ocean. But a long days" worth of work behind me, an evening and early morning of catching up on correspondence and—like the White Rabbit—I'm late! At 8:35am I realise the eclipse has already started. Throwing on clothes I rush outside. From the end of my garden, which is of a reasonable size, formed of three terraces and south facing, I can see the disk of the sun in the clear morning sky. A disk with some of its area missing. It took a second, especially in my somewhat hazy state, to fully recognise that this is it. The observable movement of one celestial body across another, an eclipse.

Years ago, in 1999, I'd worked with a small group of occultists (including Greg Humphries) on a series of pieces of magical work in the run up to the total eclipse, which passed over England, much of Europe and into India, in August of that year. While the magic had all gone well the moment of the eclipse was hidden from us by the Cornish clouds. So here I was 16 years later, actually witnessing one. Though this would not include a period of totality some 90% of the sun would be occluded over Devon.

I grab a few things; incense, a warm Nepali blanket, and the black mirror made for me by Levannah Morgan. In the absence of special glasses or some other ruse this would have to be my way of observing the event.

I climb up onto the roof of my garden studio, throwing down a few wizened apples dropped by the trees in the orchard. I wrap the blanket round me and invoke the force of an ally spirit, exhaling smoke down across the mirror and up towards the darkening sun. The trance established I stare down, my head bowed as though in prayer, so that I can look into the mirror that I hold, facing the sun, on my chest. There, in its darkness, is the crescent light, not that of the waxing or waning moon, but instead of the sun.

I widen my awareness, looking up directly at the eclipse, I am deeply aware that I witnessing our binary planetoid passing some 238,855 miles away, orbiting between the part of the globe I'm sitting on and our star. 'The Sun is God!' said J. M. W. Turner and in many respects he was right. Almost all life on earth is dependent on the sun and while our current theories suggest that the first life-forms were powered by chthonic hydrogen rather than sunlight, 4.5 billion years into the story of life on earth, most species have made the switch to solar energy. The sun, that marvellous star which each year allows our planet to bask in 3,850,000 exajoules of energy. That great mass 332,946 times heavier than the earth, which by some improbable luck appears as the same apparent size as the moon when observed by a curious ape upon the surface of the earth. I wonder, if the earth were scaled up to the size of the sun how large I would be, or if I remained my current size, how small would I be compared to the expanded, sun-sized-earth dwelling humans? Perhaps these Wonderland thoughts are inevitable when watching an eclipse because of all that business about size and distance and maths.

I'm not the only person in my locality watching the eclipse. Some neighbours are out peering through sunlight proof glasses. Perhaps disappointed with what they can see from the ground one of the local teenagers launches a rather impressive drone into the sky. At what seems like several hundred feet up it trains its camera on the sun. 'Anything?' I shout down 'Yeah, I can see it!' comes the reply.

In the nearby housing for older people a posse of my elders are taking tea and chatting, while looking up. The background birdsong dies down, although the absence is one I don't fully notice until it starts up again as the eclipse comes to an end.

I am feeling into the web of wyrd. In this instance it is the act of watching the eclipse that locates me in the centre of the magic circle. I can feel all those connections between myself and the various spirits—spirits of people, of times, of places and of ideas. I can examine and perhaps change these connections from this nexus of trance at magical eclipse time.

As Rahu swallows the sun the air becomes cold. The shadows lengthen, and the light is, well just weird. I focus on the cold, how much colder is the vacuum of space that lies between the sun and moon? Perhaps I use some of this cold power to cut off things I no longer need, to slice these webs of wyrd as the moon slices up the sun.

Alchemical Wedding

Rituals for transformation of experience that arise from desire (aka results magic) always need to be handled with care. Michael Staley, of Typhonian OTO fame, once wisely observed that magick is, in some respects, a deeply unreliable tool for doing things in the universe. In context of results magic terms, we know a spell can easily have a) exactly the effect you wanted or b) exactly the opposite effect you wanted or c) no effect at all. Would you, Mick asked, be happy to use a gun which behaved like that?

The trick to making results magic work is to spend time tuning in to what Staley called 'the subconscious', or perhaps our (True) Wills, the Tao or whatever. Explorations like mine at this eclipse are about this. They are opportunities to plug into the universe and help us build our souls. While there are times when our desires are such that we need to act, to do results magic, we need to do so from a wise place that pays attention to the tides of the 'subconscious' that we seek to ride. Practitioners who fail to do this simply do the same spell again and again, ignoring the lessons when their results fail, and taking great glee when there is an apparent result, which has more to do with confirmation bias and regression toward the mean than any sorcery.

Learning results magic, or gaining siddhis is all very well but if magic really works it means a lot more about the human condition than merely the value of masturbating over a sigil to get a bigger car, or the utility of stabbing a poppet in the hope that a foe be harmed Magic can help us connect with the spirits of life, of love, of death, of transformation. It asks much bigger questions of us than 'what do you want today?' And while the techniques, sometimes imagined as being of 'higher' and 'low' magic are much the same in structure, the intention, or desire, of one is much bigger than the other (in much the same way that the sun and moon look identical sizes, whereas this is far from the truth). The competent magician, in my view, is one who focuses much of their time on this big scale stuff. It's not a firm division; some 'high magic' also looks like 'results work', in terms of personal psychological transformation and transmogrification.

Although magic may not be an effective mechanism for getting your wish-list of desires done, it is however a great way of putting you in touch with your desiring self, so you can tune into and transform that. The wise magician is thus someone attuned to context. It makes sense to use magic to aid your healing powers if you are a doctor, nurse or carer. Learning to use magic to extend the limits of our achievable reality is where really good (i.e. successful) results magick flourishes, not in the equivalent of railing at the moon not to swallow the sun, or shooting bows and arrows at the lightning.

The Cheshire Cat grin of the crescent sun opens up like a large smile, the light begins to flood back onto the earth and onto me. I take a photograph of the mirror and send it to Levannah. She is on top of a hill in Devon, having been Sitting Out all night to await the eclipse this morning. Electronically we are connected. Later that day I send messages of greeting to many other friends. Because, in that moment, as I send a text message to Levannah, I am struck by how unbelievably wealthy I am in terms of friends, friends who are talented, beautiful, caring, fun and more.

Artha, one of the Four Noble Goals of Hinduism, is 'acquisition of wealth' and while I'm mindful of the teaching of Atu X and Bill Hicks that 'it's just a ride', I'm grateful that in this moment of power, as the sun is released from the grip of the snake, I can truly feel the warmth of a wealth that enriches my soul.

Walking in the Silence of Spring

Thoughts on the Psychogeographic Way.

For me psychogeography (or less formally, 'going for a walk') is a key practice. By moving through the landscape in a suitably mindful way, one can use the journey to explore both the inner and outer landscape. I made a journey recently, walking beside the great river that forms the valley in which I live.

At the outset I'm impressed by the weather. On this occasion there is an unusual stillness in the early spring; the river forms a silver mirror to the high grey sky above. A few wading birds explore the shallows, dipping for their food, and silent gulls row through the motionless air.

Turbulent river made still

As I walk my mind picks over recent events, as in a dream, processing and probing experiences in order to put them in place. These events included an opportunity to explore ways in which visitors to historic sites engage with the objects in those collections. The National Trust had invited me to speak at their conference and I was pleased to find that a rather lovely sign had been produced to direct delegates to my presentation.

Sign of the times

A few days later I was in the Ashmolean Museum with its world class collection of wonderful things. Visiting a museum is a chance to enter a Shrine to the Muses. These are places in which to be inspired, though one should be mindful of the ethical issues that some museum collections represent; in Britain, many objects in some of our national museums were acquired within the context of colonial imperialism.

Jai Ganesha!

Walking on. Catkins stand watch as the spring rises, and gorse glows yellow gold at the edge of the wood. It tastes sweet and alive. Having walked through the outskirts of my home town, I turn off the path and into some woodland. Here memory gives way to the immediacy of the surroundings. A stand of pine trees rises up, creating a soft woodland floor of needles. This yielding leaf litter is punctuated by the first furled forms of Lords and Ladies, *Arum maculatum*.

I spend time with the pine spirits. Often overlooked as being not as cool as broadleaf trees, I am captivated by their repeated fractal forms. I am deeply aware that these are living beings. Alive and aware of the world just as I am, in their own tree-ish way.

As well as our commonality I wonder about our differences. While it's clearly not about better or worse it does seem that my awareness is different from that of the tree. I wonder about the common religious suggestion that humans are somehow specifically created in the image of God and reflect that aside of the obvious anthropocentrism this is because we are deeply self-aware. The development of this egoic boundary is perhaps both our connection to the divine, as the embodiment of God, and the cause of our Fall—at least according to some paradigms.

I run my hands over the bark and collect some of the resin exuded by the pines. This locally and freely gathered incense is perfect for the ritual of purification I'm planning to do (that is, spring cleaning my home). I quiet my mind. The trees speak and I listen to them.

Later, on my return, I stop to gaze at the river and my memory drifts back to the death of my Dad that happened in December of 2014. At a good age, and after a brief illness, I was able to be by his side in his last days. I was blessed with a kindly, caring father and in my own way I hope that I can honour his memory by being a good parent myself and in the work that I do. Once a close loved one dies something very interesting and powerful happens. As their individual narrative ends so the relationship that one has with that person becomes a relationship with The Ancestors. My Dad has become part of that archetype of The Father and I am fortunate that we had a good relationship while he was alive. This allows me to find healthy and beautiful ways to now connect with that psychic structure. Wrathful Jehovah and his kin may be part of The Father archetype too, but my pathway to this force is now guided by the psychopomp of the kindly man whose large hand I held as the warmth evaporated from it. While I undoubtedly feel a sense of loss and of sadness, I also know his body was tired out. The soul of the man I knew has been liberated from its outworn shell and is become part of that Great Spirit.

Turning back to home I can't resist the temptation to again cut away from the path and ascend several hundred feet to the crest of a rolling Devonian hill. Great beech trees stand sentinel over the rising green earth, and gnarled oaks ride like *Hagazussa* on the dry-stone walls marking the boundaries of grazing lands.

This exertion galvanises me, and I return home to work, refreshed by my walk, inspired and enthused. For me this walking is an act of magic, an everyday magic, where we use skilful means to process those things that have been rattling around in our minds. The walk, be it pilgrimage or situationist dérive, gives us a literal new perspective, it shakes up and smooths out our psychic selves, as well as exercising our physical bodies.

It reminds us, away from our books, and screens, and other people, of all those other beings in the world; sky, birds, river, pine, gorse and more, and gives time for us to take their counsel.

My First Trip

An account of my first adventure into psychedelic space, first published in Psychedelic Press Journal.

My first chemically mediated, fully psychedelic experience happened when I was 21. I say 'chemically mediated' because well before that time I'd been experimenting with altered states. As a young man I played around with pranayama, did plenty of yoga (often sitting in the lotus position or other asanas while watching TV) had explored visualisations (with the Hindu tattva symbols, Qabalistic guided visualisations or 'pathworkings') and ritual (from candle magic spellcraft through to group experimental Wiccan ritual) amongst other ways of changing my awareness. In fact, by the age of 15 I was already a practising member of a Wicca coven.

For as long as I can remember, I've been fascinated with magic. And altered states—whether induced by fasting, sex, drugs, dance, ritual drama or other means—are critical components of the magical art. I also knew that one of the best-known occultists of the 20th century (one Aleister Crowley) was notorious for using, and writing copiously about, mind-bending drugs. As a budding magician, I was eager to try these miraculous chemicals.

Crowley, while arguably the most famous drug using occultist, is by no means unique. At the same period of history his magical colleagues, such as the poet WB Yeats, writer Arthur Machen and groundbreaking Western Buddhist Alan Bennett were also getting high on a variety of substances including peyote.

As a teenager, I'd devoured the hatchet-job biography of *Crowley The Great Beast* by John Symonds. Though Symonds paints a very unsympathetic portrait of his subject, Crowley still manages to come out of the narrative, in my opinion, as one cool guy. Symonds spills plenty of ink in laying bare Crowley's substance addictions and chemical challenges. However, while I think the author's intention was to make the whole thing seem rather unappealing, the effect on me was quite the reverse.

As I mentioned above, from the age of 15, to my mid-20s, I was doing ceremonial ritual magic with other people. This was during the 1980s, and so the older members of the groups I was part of, like most alternative/bohemian/hippy/whatever types, were familiar with both cannabis and LSD.

Before my first trip I'd tried marijuana. At first all I found was that I'd feel weird and then, if I persisted, spin out and go to sleep. But later, as I grew more familiar with the herb—its various means of administration and the concept of set and setting—I began to enjoy that complex constellation of effects we know as 'being stoned'. I'd even begun to experience a few psychedelic moments, especially when smoking outside in nature. Later I would discover that cannabis bred with a high THC content produced in me a wonderful high that, depending on dose, set and setting, could be turned up towards a genuinely psychedelic state. Cannabis was the first drug that I got a taste for. I've never been that excited by alcohol, though I have explored that substance ranging from the 'nice glass of wine with a meal' experience through to the 'heroic dose' of incoherent laughter and head down the toilet purging.

Inspired by Crowley, and informed by the writings of Aldous Huxley and others, I knew that it was the psychedelics that interested me. Sure, the romantic idea of snorting coke sounded great, and reclining on a divan while battered on opium seemed just dandy, but it was those mind-manifesting chemicals that made books glow like gems and the kind of visions described in occult literature actually happen—that was what I wanted.

Although as I have said I was around people experienced in the use of LSD, and who still occasionally used it, I didn't take the opportunity to give it a go. That chance would come following a London Pagan event. This was a pub moot by the name of Talking Stick organised by a powerful group of witches 'The Temple of the Midnight Bimbos' (really). The moot was a social event; an opportunity for pagans and occultists of various stripes to get together, discuss, argue, listen to lectures and get mildly drunk together. It was great.

Such moots formed essential glue to the emerging pagan and occult scene in the 1980s. This was an age when Pagan 'zines (collaboratively produced, mutually supportive, desk-top published and photocopied magazines) provided the primary communication tool for a community that now networks online through social media.

I don't recall the exact nature of the moot that night. It may have been some kind of a question and answer session with various luminaries being asked their views about some topic or other. I got to speak because, while only a young man, I'd already written articles for Pagan magazines and had, for better or worse, an encyclopaedic knowledge of occulture. I'm not sure what I said but what I do recall is that after the talks were done and the informal part of the event was underway, a man came up to me.

"I think you need this..." he said.

I looked at the squares of paper in his hand.

"Acid." he explained.

I hid away that powerful medicine, for a full year. The time just never seemed right. But one day the house was quiet, my then girlfriend and her son were away for the weekend, and I determined that this was it. Time to enter into heaven or hell and take the damn stuff!

Remember I already had five years' experience of group ritual practice (often as the leader or co-facilitator of a coven) and so before I took the drug I made a point of setting up the ceremonial environment. I'd also read Leary's observations about set and setting, and knew how the direction of a trip could be influenced by music, lighting etc. I had a bath and put on fresh clothes, put new candles in the candlesticks and lit some cleansing incense. I didn't formally cast a protective magic circle even though this was my usual ritual practice. On reflection this may have been a mistake.

I'd kept the acid in a wooden box. One of those little hippy style ones with brass repoussé decoration. I slid the lid back and there were these two mysterious squares of paper. I took one out and looked at the yin-yang design on it. I reasoned that the drugs had been kept out of the light and at a reasonably constant temperature but even so some of their potency would have evaporated. Still, erring on the side of caution, I used scissors to cut the first square into two triangles and ate one of them.

I listened to some music and sat around for a bit. Nothing, no hallucinogenic fireworks or divine revelations. So I took the other half.

I listened to more music, sat around a bit more. The evening sun faded in the west. Was it working?

No.

Well that's kind of a relief. Looks like these are duds. Whatever psychedelic wonderland I'd been promised had, literally, evaporated. The blotting paper I'd eaten was just that, just paper. Slightly metallic tasting paper. Oh well, next time I guess. Still; perhaps if I take the other square I may get some effect...

So I ate that one too.

Now one of the problems facing me that night was that without a wiser person to guide me I'd just made a serious error. You see what I thought was 'one' was in fact 'four', the trips having been designed so that the yin-yang was printed onto a square of four perforated blotters. I completely missed the perforations and, with no understanding of how big acid was I'd just taken 8 tabs.

Something was happening, something outside of my control. While I'd experienced altered states in magical practice most of these states can be interrupted by stopping or changing the practice. Meditation getting too weird? Go and get some food to 'earth' yourself and then chop wood for a few hours, you'll feel fine. Odd effects from that invocation of Pan last night? Take a cleansing bath and get a good night's sleep. But this felt different. I wasn't, it seemed, in control. It, the acid, was happening to me.

The darkening room began to be infiltrated by my anxiety in the form of sensed wave of inky black energy. I was worried, especially as I began to suspect that those perforations may have marked where you were supposed to rip off the individual doses of acid.

In common with many humans I'm something of a worrier and at that moment all my fears of Huxley's 'Hell' began to gnaw at the edges of my consciousness.

Then the spider came out from under the sofa opposite me. A very, very big spider.

These days I'm on pretty good terms with spiders but in that moment the sudden appearance of what I perceived as an incredibly swift-moving and gigantic arachnid sent shivers up my spine.

I leapt out of my chair, propelled by the power of my reptilian brain. The spider sat still, its body rigid. I held my breath and looked at it. I stepped closer to it. It remained immobile.

"I'm sorry spider." I heard myself say.

I brought my hand down, flat and hard, and killed it.

"I'm sorry spider, but by killing you I banish all the fear in this trip." It was like I was hearing a recording of myself. There was a dispassionate distance about the scene.

At that moment the trip kicked in proper and I found myself surrounded by a silver web of visual-tracer threads. These were immediately apparent if I closed my eyes or held them half -open. Even as I gazed around the room the objects in my field of vision seemed to scintillate silver. Everything looked so strange and so beautiful.

I sat on the sofa and reached up my arms, the angle of my limbs reminding me of the now dead spider. Poor thing! The next I remember was finding myself walking on all fours round the room, crawling in jerkily, precise movements, just like a spider. I tried crawling up the walls and moving round the space. My childhood dream of being Spiderman was being realised, I was incarnating the spider spirit.

The rest of the trip—which lasted a good twelve hours—was magnificent. I experimented with listening to a variety of music (yes to Pink Floyd, Talking Heads not so much), with yoga and dance, but mostly with drifting off into the impossibly magnificent closed eye visuals. I travelled through the Qabalah, one of my favourite metaphysical maps, swinging around the sephira, following Hermetic pathways through the conceptual iconography of Western magic.

Some hours later I found myself staring out the French windows at the garden. In the bright dawning light the trees had a mandala-like quality, each perfect and pulsating with meaning, pregnant with power. I wept at the beauty of it all.

As the effects of the acid began to wane, I began to reflect on my trip. I remembered the spider and went to look for its crushed body by the sofa. I wanted to bury it, to ask for forgiveness, to come to terms with the fact that, in what was essentially a ritual, I had sacrificed an animal and, moreover, not even one I was intending to eat.

But when I got there the spider was gone. No sign at all. To this day I don't know if it was real, or simply a projection of my fear into a visual hallucination. Either way I spent some time meditating on what had happened and came to a psychological space that felt okay to me if not necessarily for that particular spider—whether real or imagined.

It would be another nine years before I started to formally combine entheogens with my magical practice, and looking back I'm really glad I had that grounding in occultism before starting to explore drugs. But that's just my story, not a recommendation for anyone else. My experience with altered states and internalized cosmologies of the Qabalah, the tarot and the Wheel of the Year provided me with a conceptual framework for my visions, and I think that helped keep me in a good space in the face of what I now estimate was a 600 µg dose of LSD.

And while the spider may have been more imagined than real I still feel bad that I killed it. But I also recognised that what I did made total sense in that context and indeed felt like something that came through me rather than a properly premeditated act. I'm also glad that I feel bad because it is that compassion for other beings that works to prevent magic become the dull solipsistic pursuit of ego-centric power. If all things are connected then truly no man is an island. Self and other may arise as necessary elements of cognition but at a much deeper level these separations are illusory. In that sense, what I killed that night was my own fear, my fear that the drugs would overwhelm me. By becoming the spider, and finding it vanished in the morning, I absorbed that lesson into myself at a deep level.

I still get nervous before a powerful psychedelic experience, but I now know that I don't need to kill my fear. In fact, that fear can be transformed into excitement, it can be accepted and I can let it pass over me and through me. I thank the spirit of the spider for this lesson, and the spirit of LSD for opening its wonders to me that night. Lastly, I thanks that man (whose name I never knew) who gave me the medicine, and I also thank the spirit of the Trickster who arranged to give me such a good solid dose on my first trip.

Enchant Long...

The relationship of time to magical causation and prediction.

The maxim to 'enchant long and divine short' is one of the many bits of wisdom from the work of Pete Carroll. The suggestion is that if we want to create magical effects, we're generally better off casting our desires into the reasonably distant future, into situations where there are lots of variables that might be tweaked by our spells. Meanwhile divination is best done 'short'. As with predicting the weather, which can prove reasonably successful a few days ahead, whilst long-range forecasts, especially over larger areas, are often no more accurate than simple guesses. While flashes of insight can and do occur for the skilled diviner, divination tends to be primarily about assisting the querent to reflect on their own circumstances at the moment of the reading, and to empower them to understand their possible options in a given situation.

If we consider a Left-Hand Path (LHP) style of magic the injunction to 'enchant long and divine short' can result in some interesting ethical effects. Let's take the example of long-term enchantment. We know that we change over time and, whilst it's true there is a 'narrative centre of gravity'—to use a term borrowed from phenomenology and hermeneutics—our needs, desires and our identities can and do change. With this in mind, a long-term enchantment requires the magician to see the problem (their desire) not in terms of the (immediate) self but as part of a much bigger picture. This transforms what can initially arise as a grasping, outcomes-driven personal need, into something greater and more inclusive.

As an example; a couple of magician friends of mine, some years ago, were diagnosed with viral hepatitis. This is a blood-borne infection for which, at the time they contracted the virus, there was no known cure. Obviously as magicians we wanted to address this problem; and while sometimes 'miraculous' healing does take place (in my experience this often manifests itself as the patient discovering that they have been 'misdiagnosed' and that the illness that threatened has literally vanished, apparently because it was never there), it's best to take advice from Mr Carroll and learn to play the long game.

In this instance the work that we pursued was not limited to healing our friends but instead focused on finding a cure for hepatitis. As antiviral technology developed it also became necessary to perform other work, affecting the cultural and financial side of the pharmacological industry. There was, for example, one period when two firms were peddling rival drugs that actually worked best when taken in combination. The long-term result of this work (and that of the medical research profession) is that both my friends are now thankfully clear of the hepatitis virus and all the health problems associated with that infection; as are many hundreds of others.

While it's impossible to be certain whether our muttering of spells, invocation of spirits or deployment of magical cling film (Saran Wrap) helped these scientific developments (we can't of course re-run a control experiment of this bit of medical history where we don't do the magical work) the bottom line is my friends are now healthy and well. The bigger benefit is that tens of thousands of other people on the planet are well too, and it's this process that lifts the 'narrow' desire-oriented LHP style magick into something that looks much closer to a Vajrayana path; we use our own personal desires for specific outcomes or for illumination/enlightenment, and skilfully deploy these in order to achieve an outcome where all beings become liberated.

When you're doing 'results magic' for yourself why not consider how to play the long game and if there is a way of getting not only what you want but helping many others into the bargain? The example above involving healing magic is ideal; rather than working simply for your own or your client's health, consider all those others who share the same problem. Conversely when doing divination, rather than trying to scry the actions of complex networks, focus your questions on what you or the querent can do in a given situation. Considered through the lens of a left-hand path approach any divination will emphasise personal responsibility, empowerment and agency.

Perhaps this allows us to expand Carroll's dictum to: 'Enchant long and global, divine short and personal'. In works of enchantment let go the individual desiring self, consider the bigger context of your magick and, by skilful means, get much more bang for your esoteric buck. In works of divination give up the illusion that you are without agency and discover the most empowering way to adapt to the situation in which you find yourself in this moment.

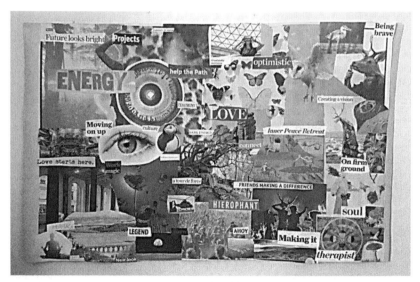

Magical collages

Season of the Spiders

Animal spirits are all around us if only we take the time to notice.

Autumn comes to the valley in which I live. The warm sunshine is still with us, Sunna be praised!, but the pivot point of the September equinox has passed. Mist shrouds the trees in the morning, the leaves of the willows fill up with yellow and fall down upon the moist green earth.

This is the season of the spiders, when these miraculous beasts spin their webs between the dying stems of grasses. In common with many humans I deeply admire the tenacity and technical skill of spiders. I watched one recently in a still-scented honeysuckle bush, dealing with a yellowed leaf that had become entangled in its web. She (I usually think of spiders as 'she') carefully made fast some gossamer lines, then ran new strands from her spinnerets and carefully cut other silks. The leaf went swinging out from the face of the web, dangling, quite literally, from a thread. Then she sat for a while, me watching intently to see if she would slice the final connection. She didn't, and looking down, I could imagine why she had stopped. The leaf hung now away from the prime killing zone of her trap, it was no longer an impediment to her. Had she cut the final strand there was a distinct possibility that the leaf would have become caught on one of the lower main strands supporting her web. If the leaf landed in this position it would have been very hard to remove, and she could have risked the structural integrity of the whole network. Instead she chose to let this now minor irritation stay, making a calculation between risk and benefit and deciding she had done enough.

As in the fabled story of Robert the Bruce, the spider is an instructor. The spider I observed was teaching an approach to the things in your life that are irritations, things that get in your way. These things may be social issues (your tiresome ex-partner is still obsessively bad-mouthing you), physical difficulties (you notice that your back problems are getting worse, inevitable as you age) or more esoteric challenges. The lesson of the spider (in the honeysuckle) is that you don't always need to finish the job. Sometimes good enough is simply good enough. If you've already done all that's needed to get your irksome ex out of your circle of friends, if you're doing exercises aimed at strengthening your poorly spine, and so on, then that may be sufficient. Save your energy for what matters (in her case sucking the life blood from flies) and strengthen your core. Don't waste attention on doing more than that which is good enough, especially if, by trying to completely resolve the problem, you risk ending up with diminishing returns or even upsetting what you have already achieved.

Araneus diadematus *hangin' out*

Meanwhile inside my house another lesson from the spiders. A voluptuous garden spider had spun her web right across my kitchen window while I was away at a conference. Upon my return I noticed her handiwork, a lovely circular web of almost Platonic perfection. While I do groove on that goth style, I was minded to remove her; until I considered the implications of doing so. On my windowsill, which is pretty deep, it being an 18th century building, sit a number of pot plants. These include *Aloe vera* (essential medicine for minor burns), various exotic cacti and more delicate species. One in particular is very susceptible to insect attack (this beautiful herb reproduces by getting humans to make cuttings of it, and rarely flowers or sets seed). So why move my arachnid guest, especially when she is protecting my indoor garden?

Another spider that made an appearance in my living room last night was a giant house spider. As autumn arrives so the males of this species leave dark their and unmolested webs in the corners of buildings. They race across the prairie of the room in the hope of finding a mate. We only really encounter these chaps when they get stuck in the bath. Whether spotted in the tub or on the prowl along the floor there is a tendency for folk to capture them and 'set them free' in the garden. This reaction is understandable. We think of our homes as ours, they are the modernised caves in which we dwell. We've bought and paid for them and any other living things inside (pets, plants, children etc) are there because we've put them there. Spiders are also, for possibly evolutionary reasons, creatures that many of us are nervous of. Best get their weird eight-legged freaky forms out of our house.

Here again the spider has a teaching: that all our spaces are in fact shared. Whether we're talking about the immense amount of microbial life that swarms inside and upon our bodies, the dust mite denizens of our beds, or our much bigger (and therefore more obvious) eight-legged housemates, we are actually surrounded by other lifeforms all the time. There are very few environments in which humans find themselves where other life forms don't exist—there are perhaps even bacteria on the outside of the international space station as well as those in the guts of the crew. You're never more than a couple of metres away from an insect and the very air we breathe is seething with bacterial beings. As far as spiders are concerned, several species are specifically linked to human dwellings. We are part of nature, we make and shape habitats, and in any given environmental niche lifeforms will find a foothold, including our buildings; fleas, silverfish, rats, pigeons, foxes, hawks, mice... and more.

While some of us might imagine that we have few dealings with other creatures in our day-to-day lives, if we stop and look, other non-human persons are all around us. These facts are one of the considerations that makes that old chestnut— that modern pagans are necessarily cut-off from nature— quite untenable. We can learn, from the attercop racing across the kitchen floor, that this is his territory too. Paying attention to our needs, as I did with the arthropod that now protects my house plants, we can often enter simple, mutually beneficial relationships. And as we observe and interact with these beings, these spirits, we can learn from their wisdom.

On Having a Girl's Aura

Explorations of gender and the magical androgyne.

Sometimes I get mistaken for a woman, and for years have explained jokingly that this is because 'I have a girl's aura'.

When I was a teenager this happened fairly often. I remember once being at a David Bowie concert in London during his Glass Spider tour. With my hair spiked in homage to Aladdin Sane and eyeliner, I guess it wasn't that surprising that the blokes sitting behind myself and my (female) partner remarked; 'Cor look! Lesbians!' However only a few years later I found myself walking with another female friend in Cumbria and something similar happened. Striding up the hillside towards Grisedale Tarn—which I always imagine as the kind of body of water beneath which a Cthuloid god may well lie dreaming—we were met by a gentleman walking the other way. Despite the fact that I had short hair, no make-up, probably stubble, a men's waxed Barbour jacket, combat trousers and boots (as did my companion) he still greeted us with a hearty 'Good morning ladies!'

And it's not a phenomenon limited to a Western, English speaking cultural context. Once when passing through airport security in India, having gone through the metal detector, I stood in front of the male security guard and lifted my arms for a pat down search. Despite being taller than the guard (I'm 5 foot, 8 inches tall) and us being face-to-face (me wearing jeans, t-shirt and no makeup or other insignia usually thought of as feminine) he directed me elsewhere. 'Ladies to go here please!' he remarked, indicating that I needed to be searched by the female guard (as would be appropriate were I a woman). I've also found these misapprehensions are not age dependent; there have been numerous occasions in which I've overheard a child taking about 'that lady', meaning me.

While clearly not a banner-headline masculine bloke (I'm rather far from the Pipe Bear phenotype) the majority of the time these situations have arisen while I've been dressed in 'traditional' male clothing and had short hair. It's interesting to consider these misapprehensions in the light of the fact that I do identify as a bisexual male, who likes a spot of cross-dressing, and a somewhat fey goth style. defence It's also interesting to note that the misinterpreting person often ends up profusely apologizing—as though mistaking me for a female is something I'd find offensive—also an interesting reaction.

There's much one could explore about these misapprehensions. Firstly, are they actually mistakes? Are those folks who 'misunderstand' me as a woman actually detecting some of these 'feminine' aspects of who I am, even when they are not being overly signalled by context, dress etc? More broadly these 'mistakes' make me aware of, and call into question, the relationship between genetic sex, genital shape, cultural norms and so on. The issues that this misinterpretation raises are subtle, fluid and multiple.

Personally, I take these misreadings of my gender as a compliment. I generally find women more attractive (at least visually) than men and so I'm always a little flattered by these 'mistakes'. More generally there may well be some kind of cultural feedback loop from my apparent 'female side' or social role (I frequently get to be 'honorary girl/woman' etc at various female-only events, such as Hen Parties).

As a magician I'm interested in these experiences because of the significance of the androgyny in pretty much every esoteric tradition. Whether it's the dual form of Ardhanarishvara, the appearance of dual-sexed imagery in alchemy, or its modern re-visioning in the chimeric sexuality of Baphomet, the notion of both genders being present in one body is a central motif in much of occulture.

I like to imagine that these misapprehensions of my apparent gender spring from what one might (in a positive sense) describe as my being 'a bit *ergi*". This was a term of abuse in Viking age culture, specially referring to a male homosexual who is penetrated anally by another man. The word was also apparently applied to effeminate men who may also be implied to have engaged in seiðr. We know little of these practices from historical sources, but which many conjecture seiðr included magic of a dark-feminine, mediumistic, sorcerous (perhaps manipulative) sort. The All Father Odin obtained the runes after nine days and nights hanging from the World Tree. In another act of extreme physical sacrifice, he gave up his left eye to The Well of Wyrd (*Urðarbrunnr*), thus acquiring *seiðr*, which is regarded as women's magic. As a *seiðmenn*, even Odin was taunted as *ergi* by Loki (*Lokasenna* 24). In some respects, *ergi* seems to be much like the complex modern word 'queer'. Today we might talk about 'receptive' qualities; the ability to listen to others/the unconscious/the spirits, and indeed to take the gods inside ourselves (with the obviously implied sexual imagery) in trance work and invocation. These seem like essential skills for the well-rounded magician, whatever their gender. If you want to explore a more nuanced analysis of *ergi* I recommend reading *Nine Worlds of Seid-Magic* by Jenny Blaine.

Perhaps it is indeed my 'girl's aura' that foxes people about the set of chromosomes I carry; maybe they unconsciously register the currents of my magical work, consisting as it does in large part of a chaos-Baphometic-witchcraft which is, frankly, pretty 'queer', or maybe it's just that I'm a lot more camp_than I generally notice, following from which there is the complex issue of whether camp behaviour is in any way intrinsically linked to the mannerisms of women, or is something else entirely...

At the altar of Pomba Gira of the Seven Crossroads

Tripping Out:
Towards a Psychedelic Psychogeography

An essay written for a French language journal of psychedelic science and culture.

Psychogeography emerges as an avant-garde strategy to disrupt dominant narratives within urban spaces and reveal hidden relationships. Whether through the open-ended play of the dérive or through the deployment of specific techniques such as navigating one city with the map of a different one, or tossing a coin to randomly select which route to follow.

As psychogeographical practice strides into the 21st century it (appropriately enough) detours and deviates in many ways. Professor of Contemporary Performance at the University of Glasgow, Deirdre Heddon, describes an 'autotopography' where the identity of the walker is generated by and reflected in the landscape. Meanwhile, in southern Britain, at the University of Plymouth Dr Phil Smith expounds a 'Mythogeography' which "... emphasises the multiple nature of places and ways of celebrating, expressing and weaving them."

While the experimental and exploratory nature of psychogeography as a whole might eschew any teleology, its broad intention could be imagined as a way to *destabilize the normal,* and to act as a tactic to *resist homogeneity of experience.*

Whether alone or in the company of others psychogeography is, as philosopher and filmmaker Guy Debord defined it; 'a mode of experimental behaviour', it is a praxis. The aim is to see the world anew. To detach from the prescribed meaning and purpose of place and do something else; to enact the deterritorialization of the territory.

Psychogeographers are agents, actors, co-creators or radical re-interpreters of their environment (the opposite of those nameless figures that populate architects' drawings, all engaged in 'approved' activities like working and shopping).

In urban settings psychogeographical eyes are drawn to the elements of our environment that are usually ignored, to aspects of our habitation that escape or challenge our usual assumptions. Rather than reading and responding to the narrative we are 'supposed' to see (according to the hegemonic discourse), our attention is instead focused perhaps on graffiti, on detritus in the gutters, on meaning interpreted from the cracks of the pavement. Psychogeographic strategies include approaches that bring our attention to the random, to chance, to the hidden or occulted aspects of our environment, the subtext or counter-text of our place.

The metropolis is undoubtedly the smog-filled cradle of modern psychogeography, but this practice need not be limited to urban environments. One's own home, the seaside, rural locations and many other places are ripe for psychogeographical investigation. All the world is a territory of meaning, offering the psychogeographer the opportunity to discover, play with, and subvert those interpretations of space wherever they may find themselves.

From its genesis in mid-20th century France, psychogeography has spawned a variety of methods for exploring, challenging and fracturing the environments we inhabit. There is 'generative psychogeography' or 'algorithmic walking' (where a set rule—take the first left and the second right, then repeat—is deployed) through to more direct interventions in a place (site specific artworks or pseudo-products smuggled onto department store shelves).

There are strategies that seek to directly challenge dominant narratives or to introduce a sense of playful curiosity and uncertainty into the space. Installing alternative signage to subvert existing public injunctions is an example of this tactic. There are dozens of examples to be found online of interventions to signage on London Underground trains. The archetypal British exemplar is the graffitied response to signs announcing that 'Bill Stickers Will be Prosecuted', to which the now-traditional repost may be added 'Bill Stickers is Innocent!'.

The legion of psychogeographical strategies includes approaches to how we move through a landscape. These methods may be deployed in combination, hybridised, selected at random, or adopted as a single tactic.

Psychogeographical practice usually involves walking (though there are strategies that might be repurposed for use on bicycles, skateboards or other means of locomotion). Certain styles of walking in itself may be deployed to enhance the exploration of the spaces we inhabit:

* Walking very slowly (particularly in a city). With long paces or as if performing a Tai Chi form (bringing attention to how the weight transfers from foot to foot).
* Walking between certain areas (from tree to tree, from one area in shadow the next).
* Adopting a particular gait—such as limping, or crouching low (to see the world as a child might).
* Walking with the balls of the feet first (rather than the heels). This manner of walking is more usual when barefoot and was commonplace before hard-soled shoes became ubiquitous.
* Walking with a zig-zagging motion.
* Selecting a route using any of the many navigation/misguiding strategies that psychogeographers have pioneered e.g. random selection of routes, following a pilgrimage path, making random marks on a map and following those, walking down roads in alphabetical order, randomly following Google searches of local features...
* etc.

We might choose to bring our attention to certain aspects of our environment:

* Simulacra.
* Reflections.
* Cracks, edges, breaks and interpenetrations.
* Weather and its effects.
* Animals (actual creatures, including humans and representations of animals) and plants (literal, symbolic and interpreted).

✳ The spaces between objects (in Japanese the Ma 間), a 'gap', 'space', 'pause'; or 'the space between two structural parts' and other lacunae.

✳ Particular colours or other foci of attention.

✳ Paying attention to smell, to other people's conversations, to the sounds of the space (as such a humming of electrical equipment or the noise of car tyres on the road). Focusing on non-visual sensory modalities.

✳ Patterns in architecture and elsewhere in the space.

✳ Walking with eyes closed, helped by a partner (the sighted person may wish to curate a 'cut up' walk for their partner of suggested textural sensations, snapshot opportunities to open their eyes, periods of stillness and listening, and so forth).

✳ etc.

To use the terminology of philosopher Hans Vaihinger—adopted by magician artist Austin Osman Spare—we can act *as if*. That is, we may choose to inhabit a role within the space (which may change our behaviour, our attention, even the way we speak). We explore the world *as if*...

✳ we are in an open air museum or gallery. taking photographs, using magnifying glasses, commenting critically on the objects we encounter and considering what they might mean etc.

✳ we are underwater.

✳ we are in hiding from the police.

✳ we are taking a last walk before our execution.

✳ we are preparing to purchase the landscape in which we find ourselves.

✳ we are considering how to embed an arts event in the location.

✳ we are a knight on a quest.

✳ we are preparing to defend the site against zombies.

✳ we are quizzical tourists from an alien world.

✳ etc.

Many of these methods are about changing our awareness, inducing what we might think of as an altered state of awareness. Humming *sotto voce* while walking is one another such trick. Humming (singing gently, chanting or even gargling) stimulates the vagus nerve (the name of the nerve itself means 'wandering' since it snakes from the brain, via the heart and lungs, to the digestive tract). Stimulation of the vagus nerve decreases the heart rate and activates the serotonin mediated 'rest and digest' functions of the body. The resulting 'trance' or 'altered state' may help the walker to become less self-conscious and more attentive to the journey rather than their own internal dialogue.

Other trance inducing sounds may also prove useful. In places where the psychogeographer wishes to retain a low profile glossolalia, for example, can easily be practiced by the simple expedient of holding a mobile phone (so that trance inducing free-form babble may appear to be simply a foreign tongue). Chanting 'found mantras' (advertising slogans or vehicle number plates) or echoing/responding to the sounds in the environment will also change our awareness. Changing the rhythm of the breath in various ways, such as breathing faster and deeper than normal with no pauses, is yet another powerful way to alter our state of consciousness.

Holding the arms or hands in unusual positions while we walk changes our attention. Deliberately reaching out and touching our environment—to feel the texture of tree bark, of brickwork, of steel and glass—provides us with new sensations normally ignored in our haste to get to where we want to go. A staff or stick may aid us in the quest to move differently and also increase our range of experience as we walk.

This desire, to be fully present in the body and the sensorium, often means that psychogeographers will dress in a way intended to render them unremarkable, even invisible in the setting they inhabit. The aim, for many, will be to forget the 'self' and merge entirely with the journey. Like hunters they blend with the landscape. The internal narrative of identity is downregulated, and attention is turned outward to focus on the strange new worlds in which they dwell.

This process of turning down the narrative sense of 'I' (the 'self' we inhabit when in conversation with others) has a neurological correlate in the reduction of activity in the brain system known as the Default Mode Network (DMN). The DMN is active when we are in our waking state and are not engrossed in an absorbing external task; when we are planning the future, ruminating about the past, thinking about other people and our relations with them, or doing tasks that are 'automatic' (such as walking or even driving). It is 'default' in that, most of the time, this is the dominant active large scale brain network. Because our awareness is so often in this default (network) mode we tend to think that this state *is* 'awareness' (or perhaps 'self-awareness') and even that this 'egoic-identity' is the totality of the person we are.

There are various states of awareness in which the activity of the DMN is reduced. These include 'flow states' that arise during highly engaging activities which require significant cognitive attention. Flow states often happen to practitioners of the arts; musicians improvising or composing, figure skaters, or video editors. In these states one's self-reflexive internal monologue reduces, time dilates (the subjective effect is of time slowing down or even stopping) and the activity is conceptualised (usually afterwards, on reflection) as autotelic (having an end or purpose in itself), absorbing and pleasurable.

In *Finding Flow: The Psychology of Engagement with Everyday Life,* Hungarian-American psychologist Mihaly Csikszentmihalyi writes about those who spend significant time in this flow-orientated, decreased DMN state of awareness:

> *An autotelic person needs few material possessions and little entertainment, comfort, power, or fame because so much of what he or she does is already rewarding. Because such persons experience flow in work, in family life, when interacting with people, when eating, even when alone with nothing to do, they depend less on external rewards that keep others motivated to go on with a life of routines. They are more autonomous and independent because they cannot*

be as easily manipulated with threats or rewards from the outside. At the same time, they are more involved with everything around them because they are fully immersed in the current of life.

Naturally this is not to say that our reflexive 'I' narrative (DMN dominant) self isn't important. A well and whole individual naturally moves between multiple mental states and cognitive flexibility can be understood as healthy in just the same way that anatomical flexibility is frequently an indicator of physical wellbeing.

Changing our mind in this way has important political outcomes, as Csikszentmihalyi suggests, allowing us to become 'more autonomous and independent'. The deployment of power (in cultural terms) tends to focus on our ego-identity and on our internal narrative of who we are (the obligations and rights accorded to us through the network of social entities, of selves, that we inhabit). Through the deployment of its technologies psychogeography seeks to throw into question these narratives of self-identity and therefore also hegemonic power by changing our relationship with space. By combining movements in space with manoeuvres made internally (by consciously altering our state of awareness, generally by downregulating the DMN) we create and curate and cultivate an experience that seeks to liberate the mind from 'threats or rewards from the outside' and gives rise to a new form of psychogeographical practice.

It is this approach to psychogeography; one that considers in detail the psychological and neurological relationships between the person, their practice and the location—as well as the wider ethical, political, and spiritual impacts of this activity—that constitutes a psychedelic (literally 'mind manifesting') psychogeography.

Psychedelic psychogeography is an altered state that demands an altered State! This practice is a tactic to resist the project of the total legibility of space (attempted in the British Isles by the fiendishly detailed mapping of that archipelago, every inch of the landscape owned and recorded by the cartography of the Imperial military, by the pervasive automatic car number plate recognition systems and CCTV).

Psychedelic psychogeography resists the closure of meaning about the subject (people and other beings), instead it provides a means of autopoiesis and social resistance to the colonisation of interiority (the idea that our minds are 'known' to Google, the Tax Office, political pollsters, ourselves etc.).

Psychedelic psychogeography then is about making a journey and changing our minds as we do so, often through the use of psychedelic drugs. This is a practice with both ancient roots and more modern antecedents. Intoxicated 19th century flâneurs Thomas De Quincey and Charles Baudelaire presage the development of a psychedelic psychogeographical with their hashish and opium augmented wanderings.

Towards the end of the 19th century in 1898 it was peyote, an exotic drug from the New World, that provided A New Artificial Paradise for physician, sexologist Havelock Ellis (his title a nod to the *Les Paradis Artificiels* of Baudelaire). He records the curious changes in awareness occasioned by this plant, the principal alkaloid of which, mescaline, is a psychedelic phenethylamine (a class of substances that don't appear to exist in significant amounts in the botany of the Old World).

Ellis shared his new discovery with two poets; William Butler Yeats (who preferred hashish) and with Arthur William Symons who wrote of his peyote experience:

I have never seen a succession of absolutely pictorial visions with such precision and such unaccountability. It seemed as if a series of dissolving views were carried swiftly before me, all going from right to left, none corresponding with any seen reality. For instance, I saw the most delightful dragons, puffing out their breath straight in front of them like rigid lines of steam, and balancing white balls at the end of their breath! When I tried to fix my mind on real things, I could generally call them up, but always with some inexplicable change. Thus, I called up a particular monument in Westminster Abbey, but in front of it, to the left, knelt a figure in Florentine costume, like someone out of a picture of Botticelli; and I could not see the tomb without also seeing this figure.

Late in the evening I went out on the Embankment and was absolutely fascinated by an advertisement of 'Bovril,' which went and came in letters of light on the other side of the river. I cannot tell you the intense pleasure this moving light gave me and how dazzling it seemed to me. Two girls and a man passed me, laughing loudly, and lolling about as they walked. I realized, intellectually, their coarseness, but visually I saw them, as they came under a tree, fall into the lines of a delicate picture; it might have been an Albert Moore. After coming in I played the piano with closed eyes and got waves and lines of pure color, almost always without form, though I saw one or two appearances which might have been shields or breastplates—pure gold, studded with small jewels in intricate patterns. All the time I had no unpleasant feelings whatever, except a very slight headache, which came and went. I slept soundly and without dreams.

Note how 'The Spectacle'—in this account indicated by the advertisement for Bovril—is subverted, becoming an object of inherent fascination rather than merely the signifier of a product. Auspiciously the word 'Bovril' itself was derived from the work of novelist and politician Edward Bulwer-Lytton author of *Vril: The Power of the Coming Race* (1871). Inspired by his interest in occultism Lyton's book is an early science-fiction story featuring a subterranean race waiting to reclaim the surface of the Earth 'Vril' was a term analogous to psychic energy or *chi* and was enthusiastically adopted by late 19th century occultism and then by esoteric neo-Nazis. The 'bo' part of the name indicates that this salty meat extract is taken from beef.

Symons' psychedelic adventures beside the river Thames prefigure the intimate relationship between space, place and altered states that would emerge in the lexicon of the middle 20th century. While World War II ravaged Europe, in the neutral state of Switzerland, a new psychedelic substance was discovered that, a few decades later exploded into European culture transforming it for ever. As the first atomic bomb neared completion, research chemist Albert Hofmann inadvertently discovered what remains one of the most potent (in terms of both subjective effect and dosage range) of mind altering substances—lysergic acid diethylamide (LSD).

To take LSD is to trip. The first use of 'trip' to mean 'psychedelic experience' appears in the late 1950s. It may have been coined by US Army scientists during their experiments with this drug (according to *Acid Dreams* by Martin Lee) but like lysergic acid itself the 'trip' soon escaped those military compounds, finding its way into underground culture. In 1964 Ken Kesey and his LSD-taking Merry Pranksters bought a school bus in the name of Intrepid Trips, Inc. *The Routledge Dictionary of Modern American Slang and Unconventional English* claims:

> *Kesey wrote about his recollection of the first use of the term: "I think it came from our bus trip in 1964, when (Neal) Cassady said 'This trip is a trip.'"*

The following year the word 'trip' appeared as a synonym for 'drug experience' in songs by Donovan, Bob Dylan and The Rolling Stones. 'Trip' was both a noun (what happened when you took or 'did' LSD) as well as the name for the squares of blotting paper on which LSD was dropped. 'Trip' was also a verb—to 'do' LSD was 'to trip'.

There is undoubtedly a similarity between psychedelic experience and physically travelling. Even before the advent of LSD European writers had described psychedelic experience in terms of a journey (novelist Norman Mailer uses the word 'trip' when relating his experience with mescaline in 1959, though the word is used metaphorically and not as slang). But outside of the Euro-American world the interpretation of psychedelic experience as a journey is common to many cultures with a tradition of using these substances (such as the Mazatec people of Mexico who make use of psilocybin mushrooms, morning glory and *Salvia divinorum*). In these communities the ritual specialist takes psychedelics to 'travel'; to find what has been lost, to search for healing, to visit and bring back wisdom from imaginal worlds.

Whether this 'psychedelic' altered state of awareness is generated by consuming a plant or potion or induced by other means such as drumming, fasting, or chanting the metaphorical journey, a 'trip', lies at the core of what is usually described as 'shamanic' practice.

In his classic text on the subject *Shamanism: Archaic Techniques of Ecstasy* Mircea Eliade repeatedly refers to the 'ecstatic journey' of the shaman. This journey often includes a specific (psycho) geography that unfolds in the imaginal world during trance:

> ... *the master (shaman) takes the novice's soul on a long ecstatic journey. They begin by climbing a mountain. From it the master shows the novice the forks in the road from which other paths ascend to the peaks; it is there that the sicknesses that harry men have their dwellings. After this the master takes his disciple into a house. There they don shamanic costumes and shamanize together. The master reveals to the novice how to recognize and cure the sicknesses that attack the various parts of the body. Each time that he names a part of the body, he spits in the disciple's mouth, and the disciple must swallow the spittle so that he may know "the roads of the evils of Hell." Finally the shaman takes his disciple to the upper world, among the celestial spirits. The shaman henceforth possesses a "consecrated body" and can practice his profession.*

While Eliade saw the use of 'narcotics' as "a recent innovation [that] points to a decadence in shamanic technique" this perhaps says more about his own prejudices than it does about 'shamanic technique'. With a wider ethnographic field of view it seems clear that there are many 'shamanic' cultures with ancient traditions of using psychoactive and especially psychedelic substances. Specimens of peyote discovered by archaeologists in Texas suggest this plant was used in a ceremonial context there over three thousand years ago.

In the modern west the adventure of the LSD 'trip' might also unfold primarily as an internal journey. With the increasing availability of vinyl records and stereo equipment a group of 1970s LSD enthusiasts could play suitable music to curate and guide their (nonambulatory) psychedelic adventures. In more active settings LSD would be taken at festivals, while dancing or making love, and for many users an important component of the trip would be to sally forth and find somewhere suitable to watch the sunrise. Walking out into a radically changed landscape to see the dawn became and remains a commonplace activity for aficionados of LSD.

Psychedelic psychogeography, then, is the meeting of these approaches; the deployment of psychogeographic intentions and methods combined with the use of techniques and especially substances that change awareness.

Since the middle of the 20th century various ways to combine the pharmacological trip and the literal journey have been explored. One of the better known approaches is that of taking psychedelics at a 'museum level' dose. Psychedelic chemist Alexander Shulgin writes in *Phenethylamines I Have Known And Loved: A Chemical Love Story:*

> *A commonly used term for a level that produces a just perceptible effect is "museum level." This is a slightly-over-threshold level which allows public activities (such as viewing paintings in a museum or scenery watching as a passenger in a car) to be entered into without attracting attention. There can be considerable discomfort associated with being in the public eye, with higher doses.*

Since the work of Timothy Leary et al it has been widely understood that *set* (the mindset of the person taking the psychedelic) and *setting* (the environment in which the drug is taken) are critical factors in determining how the experience unfolds. Taken outdoors psychedelics often provoke a sense of wonder and even mystical rapture, especially when used in natural spaces, wild landscapes or gardens. Populated urban environments may be more challenging (as Shulgin suggests) and this is particularly true if the person consuming the psychedelic is doing so in an unlicensed context.

Psychedelic psychogeography provides a nomadic setting for a trip which, while it may present challenges, also offers numerous opportunities. Naturally considerations of the subjective and physical effects, dosage, duration and intensity of the substances used is of critical importance.

For example psychedelic researchers and writers Gracie and Zarkov write of the drug 2-CB:

"... at this [16mg] dosage, one should find it possible to walk around a museum and enjoy the enhancement of color and an increased ability to interpret and become involved with the paintings and other forms of art. (It is not, however, advisable to visit a museum or any other place outside the home until you have a great deal of familiarity with the effects of 2C-B.)"

How psychedelic drugs and psychogeography can be combined comes with knowing the territory of both worlds—the inhabited and the pharmacological—and how they blend best together. We might, for example take a psychedelic and only turn to psychogeographical practices (going outside for a physical walk) towards the end of the trip as we are coming down (and perhaps the sun is rising).

Other ways to combine these practices are possible when shorter acting substances are used, notably the DMT family of tryptamines. When smoked these substances generate intense experiences that last only a matter of minutes. This shorter duration of effect can allow the psychedelic psychogeographer to deploy these substances, at doses significantly higher than 'museum level', perhaps at a specific point in the journey (at a place which feels suitable and secure).

The emerging field of psychedelic psychogeography blends together the inner mythic journey of the shaman with the physically of wandering the landscape. This practice may take place in urban or rural settings, at 'museum level' or at higher dose. This approach may be deployed as part of a 'pilgrimage' where participants walk between 'sacred sites' such as prehistoric megaliths, remarkable natural features—such as the confluence of rivers or unusual geological formations—or modern locations (telecommunications masts, nightclubs or shopping malls) that are interpreted in symbolic, associative terms.

When we use psychedelics within a psychogeographical practice the destabilization of 'normality' occurs at behavioural (how we walk), cognitive (how we interpret the territory), neurological (as Default Mode Network activity decreases) and mythical (as our awareness of 'the sacred' or ecstatic increases) levels. Through this approach the everyday becomes the holy. The imagined becomes the viscerally real. Experience becomes charged with multiple meanings and we move like giants across the strange landscape we inhabit.

Recommended Texts

Counter-Tourism: The Handbook. Crab Man (Phil Smith)

The Museum Dose: 12 Experiments in Pharmacologically Mediated Aesthetics. Daniel Tumbleweed

The Wanton Green: Contemporary Pagan Writings on Place. Gordon Maclellan and Susan Cross (Editors)

Walking Backwards or, The Magical Art of Psychedelic Psychogeography. Greg Humphries and Julian Vayne

Getting Higher: The Manual of Psychedelic Ceremony. Julian Vayne

Reeds that histle in the faint autumn breeze

All Shall be Well

The challenge and the power of adopting a positive frame of mind.

'It was necessary that there should be sin; but all shall be well, and all shall be well, and all manner of thing shall be well.'

Julian of Norwich

This may well be an unfashionable idea, or perhaps an unpopular belief system to enter into. But what if, everything is going to turn out fine?

The internet, and culture generally, are full of voices that are telling us that 'it's all going to shit'. Economic meltdown, increased militarism, ecological collapse, a giant meteor that's going to do away with us; in all these cases, it's just a matter of time. The End has already begun, apocalyptic visionaries of many stripes are ubiquitous. It's all going to hell in a handcart.

I've been listening to a lot of BBC Radio 4 recently, taking refuge in Melvyn Bragg's excellent series In Our Time and chortling to the ribald and yet intellectual humour of brilliant comedies such as I'm Sorry I Haven't A Clue. Meanwhile I've been inadvertently pumping myself full of news about lost sailors and missing aeroplanes. Tales of the abduction of children in Nigeria. The growing crisis in Ukraine. Slotted regularly between the fabulous opiates of The Archers and Desert Island Discs, the incessant Radio 4 news has a clear subtext—we're all fucked. The Great Decline and probably The Last Days are upon us.

At least, that's what I'm 'supposed' to think.

I've written previously about how humans are neurologically wired to remember bad experiences more distinctly than good ones. We crave those stories of what a friend of mine calls 'the problem'. There is always a 'problem'. Something is wrong, and our neurology is geared to notice this, to be attentive, to marshal cognition and muscles and language and culture, to address it. Think about it; what for you is 'the problem' now? Or to put it in another way, what is there that needs to be done next? Something, as every politician will urgently inform you, simply must be done.

But what if nothing needs doing and more broadly the world does not need either 'saving' or abandoning? What if, as the 1927 poem by Max Ehrmann Desiderata expresses it; 'whether or not it is clear to you, no doubt the universe is unfolding as it should'? Pan back in space and time for example; witness the differences that humans are making to the planet. Through the destruction of forests, the burning of fossil fuels, genetic engineering, nanotechnology, the internet, the global gradual increase in human lifespans. Grand changes indeed, but nowhere near what happened in the early earth; when the atmosphere was poisoned with oxygen by selfish genes that photosynthesised without any thought of the long-term consequences. On that basis, and given the ability of life as a whole to adapt to all kinds of environmental changes and externally visited events (like huge meteor strikes), I don't have much fear that humans will spell the end of life on this planet, no matter what we do.

'The problem' is frequently imagined to come from us humans and our relations with each other (and this is an often-forgotten point about apocalyptic visions; that they always include some form of human generated original sin). Something is wrong with people. According to some we are Godless perverts doomed to Biblical floods, for others we are debilitatingly deluded by our dangerous faith in a supreme being. Our apocalyptic commentators must find this Fall and then, through their eschatology, deliver us from evil (which is usually achieved by either going back to some imagined pristine primordial state, or else transcending the meat suit of the body).

Perhaps 'the problem' can be fixed by becoming a Breatharian and preparing to ascend into your lightbody for 2012? Maybe the Fall was industrialisation, or farming, and the answer is to prepare for a post- civilisation world (cue ninja bushcraft and archery practice)? Maybe the problem is all that Paganism in the Bible and we should start handing out copies of The Watchtower? Or if the problem is Christianity, then therefore becoming a Satanist is surely the right thing to do.

Not only are most of these discourses examples of answering the complex question of our being-in-the-world with a simplistic answer, they also often claim that 'the problem', whether through positive action or ennui, must be engaged with. According to this mindset, we need to address what's going on round here. To do any less indicates woolly-headed, naïve, fluffy quasi- New Age thinking, lacking in rigour, and courage to face facts.

Really?

I would agree that many of 'the problems' faced by our species are very real; social inequality, in my opinion, is the biggest one. However, given the story of the evolution of our planet, the development in technical capacity by humans does not by any means point to the show being over. What if things are going to work out just fine? This isn't to say that hurt, horror, pain, inequality doesn't happen. This isn't to say that everything is okay now and nothing needs to be done, to be nurtured, or to be opposed. Rather it is to take a rather grander, and simpler (less ideologically driven) position that adopts a somewhat Taoist perspective.

When people think of Taoism, they tend to imagine rather beatifically smiling tai chi teachers and jolly old wise men. That's all true of course, but there are also plenty of fascinatingly engaged and tactical expressions of this paradigm. The perception of the Way of the Tao (and one might argue the 'Way of the Wyrd' in a Western context) isn't about not acting. It's not even about not making mistakes; but it is about finding, and indeed in some sense trusting in, the Way. Trusting in the process.

The Taoist classic the *Tao Te Ching* has various things to say about politics and social relations, including advice for government ministers:

Governing a large country
is like frying small fish.
Too much poking spoils the meat.
When the Tao is used to govern the world
then evil will lose its power to harm the people.
Not that evil will no longer exist,
but only because it has lost its power.
Just as evil can lose its ability to harm,
the Master shuns the use of violence.
If you give evil nothing to oppose,
then virtue will return by itself.

John McDonald translation

What a powerful spell this Taoist-style perception is! A life-hack on our own neurology, a banishing on the Fall and its Apocalypse memes, a magic that may nurture and empower us in every sphere. What a radical (and indeed in some senses revolutionary or even 'Satanic') enchantment to cast! But this charm can't simply be deployed at a linguistic level. Transforming 'problems' into 'challenges' is all well and good (as long as we can keep our sense of humour about what we're doing). For a deeper effect giving thanks is a potent technique, as are methods such as Metta Bhavana and other means of changing our perspective on sorrow. One might build this development, of an 'active equanimity', into a ritual. Releasing our fear of the future in order to free up cognitive capacity and widen our awareness:

As your own neurology relaxes around the idea of 'the problem', so you get into that Taoist groove. Experiencing the deep understanding, the gnosis that the universe is unfolding just as it should. Being aware that, as you make contact with this paradigm, the effect on you will ripple outward, in weird astral and direct inter-personal terms, touching everyone you're in contact with. Invoking a nurturing, compassionate and engaged relationship with the world. Giving you an attentive and relaxed place from which to make judgements that open up, rather than limit, our possible futures.

For Every Complex Problem...

Keeping it simple isn't always the answer.

One of the lovely interpretations of the classic chaos glyph (that eight-pointed star thingy which itself has various names, none of which are perfect descriptions) is the idea that it represents magic expanding outwards in all possible directions. This is a symbol of diversity and multiplicity rather than a unitary simple Truth. The many-rayed sigil reminds us that, as American essayist and satirist H. L. Mencken pointed out; "For every complex problem there is an answer that is clear, simple, and wrong." In the complexity of human existence (which has, I suspect, always been pretty complex even in various imagined 'simpler' ages) what appear to be 'straightforward' answers (often served as naïve religious, philosophical or esoteric Truths) often turn out to be bunkum.

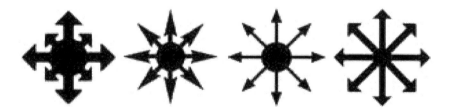

For sure, there are times when we must decisively act. When we must say 'no' and draw a line in the sand. There are times when we must slice those Gordian Knots and cut through complexity to find clarity. But the poor quality simple answers I'm thinking of are the kind of (supposedly) axiomatic articles of faith that get trotted out without much reflective thought.

Take, for example, a view that began to emerge as Freud et al. were exploring the subconscious architecture of the human mind. Some folk claim the big problem with society is that we're all sexually repressed. If only we could somehow be free sexual beings; free of the patriarchal fear of female erotic power, free of repressive laws about nudity, free of our own

Judeo-Christian notions of sexual guilt and shame. If only we could be free in this way everything would be groovy (the suggestion is that miraculously dealing with what is perceived as 'the big problem' will somehow fix all the other difficulties in culture).

While there is certainly merit in exploring the issue of sexual openness there are difficulties with the idea that a fully liberated sexuality would be a panacea. For instance, individuals who, perhaps as a result of illness, don't exhibit any sense of 'repression' end up finding life in consensus reality pretty tricky. Sexual disinhibition can arise as a result of neurological damage and for the people with these difficulties, their families and carers, the trauma caused by a reduced ability to understand what is appropriate behaviour in a given context can be greatly distressing.

This is not the same as saying that sexual mores in culture cannot and do not change. I was recently at a Cornish beach where it is accepted that people may, if they wish, go naked. (Note: Nudity is usually deemed highly unacceptable on beaches in Britain.) There has been a generally gradual social process which means that, still with boundaries, nudity is accepted in this locality. Equally we can look at the objects left by other cultures which point to the flexibility of human social mores on nudity and sexuality. Some years ago, I was involved in the curation of an exhibition and associated sexual health project that used objects from the past and other cultures as lenses through which we can explore how ideas about sexuality change. Change certainly happens, and sometimes change is sweeping and radical. But even dramatic change happens within a context, which we ignore at our peril.

When we consider simple (and wrong) solutions there's also that often quoted idea that 'if only we could live in the moment'; to deeply appreciate the now rather than being caught up in our stories of the past and future, then we'd all be so much happier (and of course society would be so much better...). But is this 'simple truth' of the power of now really, like 'love', all we need? Look at the life experience of individuals who only (as a result of neurological trauma) live only in the present. What we see are people with memory illnesses who find their situation confusing, distressing and, like those with sexual disinhibition, impossible to integrate into consensus reality. Living in the moment is great, mindfulness meditation is great, but only as part of a balanced diet of cognition that includes having plans, regrets, hopes and fears.

There's also that pervasive idea that 'all we want is to be happy'. Again, a simple solution to the complex problem of human experience. But is happiness really all we want? I had an interesting conversation on this subject with my children where we discussed whether, as a thought experiment, we would be prepared to take a pill that would make us happy for the rest of our lives. Having discussed the various problems and paradoxes involved we decided that none of us would take the happiness pill because if we did (although we'd not notice, because we'd just be happy...) we'd somehow have lost something of our humanity. Happiness is an aspiration for many of us, but a lifetime of total blissful joy—would that actually be cool? What of the context in which we are being happy? What, as James T. Kirk of Star Trek fame repeatedly observed, about the importance of struggle as part of the human condition?

For me the chaos sphere/chaos star/octaris/eightfold pointy thing is a reminder that changing ourselves and the world is a multifaceted and complex process. We need a variety of skills, of tactics, of selves and of truths. We need to take a wide view and engage with the full range of experiences available to us. Rather than take refuge in simplistic statements (whether couched in esoteric, political or other terms) that pretend to a self-evident marvellous power of radical and total transformation. The symbol of chaos reminds us that the world is complex, mutable and multiple. The eightfold star invites us to explore the full panoply of what it means to be fully human and to remember that for every complex problem...

Intent, Consequences and Virtue

As ye sow, so shall ye reap.

The use of the Statement of Intent is a common feature of many magical rituals. This can be couched in Pagan terms 'We meet here today to celebrate the festival of Samhain ...', in NLP savvy results-magick style, 'We rejoice as the project of fracking is abandoned in the British Isles' or Buddhist friendly lingo, 'We dedicate the merit of this practice to the liberation of all beings'. And though it's undoubtedly important to spend time divining and formulating what it is we want our magick to accomplish, it's also important to appreciate the rule of Unintended Consequences. There are lots of examples of this principle; the inadvertent increase in biodiversity in some war-ravaged parts of the world, or the increased use of fossil fuels as smoke-free nightclubs put heaters outside to warm their patrons now banished into the chilly night.

Living as we do, in a complex world of ever-shifting inter-connected events, the idea of framing our desires as 'I want X', ought not be regarded as the whole story by any measure. In fact, I'd suggest that most of our magick operates as much through us, as something that apparently emerges from us. In those ritual moments, where we become conscious of the process we're engaged in (celebrating Halloween, doing results magick, or a spot of Tonglen), we're actually pointing back towards the ongoing process of our lives, reminding ourselves of what we're doing just as much as casting our desires into the future.

Let's say that you do a protection ritual for someone. The way in which the ritual is framed will emerge from your psychological state at that time. Do you choose to mirror the nasty stuff coming at you, returning it to its apparent point of origin? Do you attempt some cursing sorcery or ill-wishing antics? To generalise; the former policy (setting up protective wards, working to support those who are under threat and make them stronger, deploying blocking and binding spells), betokens a much more nuanced, long-term and intelligent way of dealing with the problem than wildly stabbing at poppets or similar histrionics.

If you're a poppet stabber, chances are that you're caught up in a view of the universe characterised by fear and hatred. In such a state that old chestnut Lust of Result (assuming you think it applies in your model of magic) will probably be at a maximal value. It's also likely that the law of Unintended Consequences will get you. This isn't some kind of re-writing of karma or three-fold return but the simple fact that if you set out to do harm from this mindset, which is unable to see the bigger picture of events, you may well end up seeing your intention backfiring.

I saw a great example of this recently following the unpleasant trolling of friend where the anonymous emails sent her way galvanised a great upwelling of support on her behalf. These included messages of care and assistance from people she has previously had minor disagreements with. In swinging his metaphorical club around the troll stirred up a support group for their intended victim. This process included inadvertently calling allies with specialist computer skills, ideal for tracking down the miscreant. The actions of the nasty troll (who of course made claims of curse-wielding powers) had the unintended consequence of summoning a bunch of particularly helpful spirits to my friend's aid.

Does this cut both ways? What if you act all starry-eyed and trusting in the universe? What of the unintended consequences of becoming a doormat for those opportunistic, confused or just plain psychopathic people out there? There's no 'universal law' to stop that happening, however this is where the idea of Virtue comes in. Developing a Virtue is the deliberate cultivation of a dynamic equilibrium between extremes of behaviour. There is, for instance, the virtue of 'courage'. At one end of the continuum of behaviours we have 'foolhardiness', and at the other end 'cowardice'. Courage stands somewhere between them. By cultivating our virtue, we seek to place ourselves in a balanced, yet dynamic relationship with the world, and in practice this means we usually have a wider field of perception. We're better able to notice the unintended consequences (both positive and negative) of our actions and reactions to the world. We're more flexible and more likely to be successful in what we do (and able to address the lessons from our failures more honestly). (My favourite model of virtue is described in *Character Strengths and Virtues* by Christopher Peterson and Martin Seligman).

The person fixated on getting their way in the universe (bellowing Barbaric words at the top of their voice in the street and relentlessly pushing their monolithic interpretation of the world) is likely to be very far from virtuous. They miss the positive unintended consequences of their actions (from which they might theoretically capitalise) and the negative consequences (which could inform them to change tactics). Their obsessive desire makes them quite ignorant of what's actually going on around them and, amusingly, the more they dig themselves into their rut the easier it is for the unintended consequences—especially those that diametrically oppose what they want—to proliferate. They literally invoke their own downfall.

Both our daily lives and formal ceremonies may have all kinds of consequences, some of which we will never know (check out the excellent movie Cloud Atlas for a beautiful exploration of this idea). The aim of the wise magician then, is to cultivate an ongoing project of developing their virtue. This is a pragmatic sorcerous strategy to get us what we want. Our virtue is reflected in our spells, in what we choose to pray for, and how we choose to act in the world. Those who spend their time working to screw up the lives of others tend to end up friendless and screwed up themselves. Those who work for wisdom, justice and humanity in the world actively create the conditions for those experiences to manifest. Such people are better able to weather the storms when times get tough. Moreover, when the storm is done they've got plenty of capacity in themselves to enjoy the sun, and many loved ones around them with whom they can share it.

Talismanic replication

Finding Your Way in the Woods:
The Art of Greg Humphries

Part of my style is to collaborate with others. Of the books I've written, half have been co-authored. Greg and I released our second collaborative publication Walking Backwards Or, The Magical Art of Psychedelic Psychogeography *in 2018 and have been collaborating not only as writers but as friends, fathers, magicians and psychonauts since 1998. I am honoured to celebrate his work in this volume.*

Greg Humphries doesn't define himself as either a magician or an artist. "I call myself a woodsman", he explains. "Terms like artist and magician carry with them so much baggage, and if I'm going to do some work with someone, for example helping them learn how to coppice their woodland, then those words can create a barrier." Today, most of Greg's artistic practice looks very much like the set of skills that are typically described as bushcraft—the art and science of living successfully on the land with minimal tools. These skills have been brought into popular consciousness most recently by British experts such as Bear Grylls and Ray Mears. Both these practitioners, in their own work, have touched upon the spiritual dimension of bushcraft. Mears in particular is inspired by the reverence and intimate understanding of nature observed in many 'tribal' or 'native' cultures, attitudes required if one is to survive with some measure of success in the wilderness.

For Greg, this spiritual dimension, although strategically hidden from view by words like 'woodsman', is essential both as a personal motivator for his practice and in order to understand his own trajectory as an artist.

In 2004 Greg and I wrote *Now That's What I Call Chaos Magick: Volumes 1 & 2* (*NTWICCM*) published by Mandrake of Oxford. *Volume 2* (the second part of the book) was written by Greg. Both volumes, in complementary and yet different ways, explore our engagement as magicians with the style of occultism known as chaos magick and, more specifically, document a series of workings that we were engaged in, through different approaches, at the time; to obtain Knowledge and Conversation of the Holy Guardian Angel. Both of us had come into the orbit of the chaos magic style, and the esoteric organisation The Magical Pact of the Illuminates of Thanateros (IOT)—an occult network and esoteric laboratory environment founded in late 20th century Europe.

Before that time Greg began exploring magic and ceremonial ritual in a different style. He says:

Way back in the 1990s, in the early days of The Order of Bards, Ovates and Druids (OBOD) I was working with the Druids, wanting to find magick in some way. I did the OBOD course of study, which is a fantastic course and I really got a lot out of it. Made some really good friends and there are lots of people I'm still close to. But I found myself one day in Bristol, doing a ritual with other Druids which was about the Court of King Arthur. I asked everyone to turn up in business suits. We'd do this invocation of the power of Arthur's round table, which I imagined as this corporate style entity, the Feudal overlords, the G8 summit. I was going to incarnate the spirit of Arthur so I lay on the table doing some overbreathing techniques I'd encountered in Dave Lee's book Chaotopia. *I invoked Merlin and let my mind wander into glossolalia. I can't remember what I said (I hope the others present can!) but it seemed a fairly tame, gentle magickal ritual to me. There were others in the group who were a bit bemused by the experience, 'What has this got to do with Druidry?" they asked. I couldn't answer, as it seemed obvious to me that this was a ritual using different techniques to bring about a change in consciousness with a Druid/Celtic dressing. It was then I realized that I was trying to change the group to follow my desire to explore magick; rather than me changing I was expecting the group (and Druidry) to change to suit me, to conform to my expectations. Which is how I came to go outside Druidry and find the IOT.*

Joining the IOT really opened everything up for me. That's what chaos magick does. It's a very postmodern approach to magick; you can do anything. There isn't a single path, there are multiple paths. The IOT experience really paralleled the Master's degree in Fine Art that I did in Falmouth, because the Master's degree said the same thing. It asked me: 'What's your artistic practice about? Because you can do anything.'

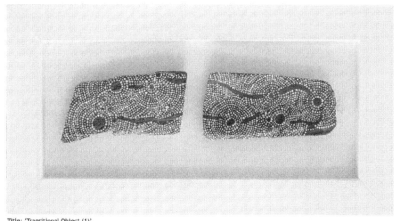

Title: 'Transitional Object (1)'.
Media: Emulsion Paint on Hartland Stone.
Artist: Greg Humphries.
47cm x 25cm x 4cm (Framed).

Transitional Object (1). Paint on Hartland Stone

During this period Greg was creating dot paintings on both canvas and natural stone surfaces. This style grew, in part, out of his engagement with South American spiritual styles— specifically the use of the entheogenic brew ayahuasca.

I was trying to find a way, an art to communicate the kind of experience I was having, particularly with ayahuasca which I think is the most amazing tool. I was in this situation where I had free reign in both my artistic and magical practice—I needed to find a way through this. I was doing the dot paintings and felt like I'd come to the end of that practice. I'd been trying to communicate through abstract art, to try to communicate some kind of spirit of nature. It's like the question that the artist John Wells asks about how you paint the experience of the warmth of the sun, so that when you encounter an artwork in the gallery it can give you that sense of the warm tingling of sun on your skin. That was why the St Ives modernist school—particularly since I was then studying, and now live, in Cornwall—is really important for me because it's about opening up to nature, the spirit or being of the place. And, it's about connecting with that spirit at a different, deeper level. So rather than being purely visual (such as a really beautiful vista of trees and mountains and so on) for me it was about how do you communicate that feeling of being in nature.

For Greg the drive to express the idea that nature isn't just a physical object, but is a spirit, a being, is reflected in his admiration of writers who are profoundly informed by place.

Tolkien, CS Lewis, Alan Garner, Alan Moore—all that literature is about opening doorways into the Otherworld, the dimension of spirit. For me, as an artist, I was on the journey to find out how I could do this. I was drawing on paper, exploring different techniques, when I started getting into bushcraft. I wanted to make bows and arrows, to learn to spin wool and knit. I didn't really understand why but that was the direction my practice was taking me in. Gradually I did less and less drawing and painting, and more bushcraft. Because for me, to really get that feeling of nature you have to physically be in nature. This brought up all kinds of questions for me; for example do you need to make art objects to be an artist? In my own artistic practice I discovered that I didn't need to make things that are explicitly art objects. Because my practice itself is about connecting people (including myself) more and more deeply with nature. For me the best way to do that is to practically work with nature in a particular environment, in a particular place. My practice looks like taking people for a walk in nature, making fire with them, foraging for wild food, making shelter. Gaining this deeper connection with nature and realising that you can be quite comfortable, even if it's raining, even if it's cold. And realising that it's okay, nature is benign, it's not out to get us.

What is sometimes called the 'Medicine Path'; the use of ayahuasca and other sacred psychoactive plants, is a vital element in this process for Greg.

These plants and the shamanic way of using them are also about opening up to those nature spirits. They teach us to open up, to relax and be able to appreciate the beauty of the universe; the sun, the moon, the stars, the trees—and that the natural world loves us.

This attitude parallels those of Ray Mears, 'Saint Ray' as Greg affectionately refers to him. In a British newspaper article Mear's is quoted:

"Nature is alive all around. It's vibrant and I enjoy being a part of it. It's difficult to explain. There's a secret life there. While we're sitting talking now, there are animals all around us, voles and mice, and the green woodpecker over there is hungry and they're moving around living their lives and we don't normally see it. But you can learn to step into their world if you know how to move quietly and be observant. You can really feel a part of what's happening. And it's magic. It's truly magical. And then you start to see patterns in nature that you see in other places. They become almost like universal truths. And then you start to trust it."

*Blowing on natural charcoal King Alfred's Cakes (*Daldinia concentrica)

How does Greg reconcile this view of the natural world as being a loving place with the perception that bushcraft skills are about a survivalist mentality?

The problem with the survivalist mentality is that it sets up an expectation that what you're really trying to do is to escape from nature. The idea is that you're going to be in this very unforgiving environment for a short period of time until you can be 'rescued' from that place and taken away. Whereas, for me, bushcraft is about learning to live with nature, and being comfortable and happy in that environment. Whether it's the Amazon, whether it's the desert, whether it's the Arctic, whether it's Devon—wherever. It's about living in, and enjoying that environment.

Greg has travelled extensively and lived close to the land in a number of locations. These include the Arctic in Norway and the Brazilian Amazon which he visited in 2007, in part in order to deepen his engagement with ayahuasca. Ayahuasca could be considered as a remarkable example of how an intimate knowledge of place can open the doors to the otherworld. The psychedelic brew, famed for producing profound visionary experiences, is the result of the cunning combination of two Amazonian plants. *Banisteriopsis caapi* (often called 'The Vine of the Soul') which gives ayahuasca 'the force', is blended with *Psychotria viridis* or 'chacruna', a leaf rich in tryptamine compounds that provides 'the light'. Given the prodigious number of plant species available in the Amazon the discovery of this combination seems quite miraculous since neither plant when ingested alone is significantly psychedelic. It is only when together they are prepared as a drink (an exhaustive process involving the laborious pounding of the vine and many days of boiling of the potion) that these plants create a chemical synergy which produces this potent ally in expanding consciousness.

Back in Cornwall now, Greg maintains both a home studio and an outdoor one. He manages six small woodlands in the local area for private clients, one of which acts as the base for the courses he runs. Greg's studio is part of a traditional smallholding in an idyllic location near Penzance, Cornwall.

It provides eco holidays, environmental education programs, courses and events. There is a roundhouse, a straw bale house and wild camping pitches. Greg was one of the team who created the buildings and is the provider of outdoor education courses at the site. These courses use the woods to connect people to the landscape. Greg and his colleagues take people into that woodland and get them to create objects made from the materials they find there. The objects made in these sessions are generally practical in nature; walking sticks, greenwood furniture, bows, arrows, tool handles, fencing panels (hurdles), charcoal etc. Greg believes these objects should be aesthetically pleasing and also have practical applications, and the link between this 'hands on' philosophy and the Arts and Crafts movement is not lost on him.

There is no spoon

Politically I feel a definite affinity with William Morris and the Arts and Crafts movement. It's a very Zen thing; the maker is in control of each part of the process from growing the tree to the finished object and every aspect of production is done with care, and with awareness—both physically and spiritually—of the process and the environment. I'm not against artworks in galleries and indeed I sometimes work within the gallery system [Greg occasionally works for Tate St.Ives] however, I'm primarily interested in artworks that are process driven and don't only have to exist in gallery spaces, but can exist also in a practical way within our lives. So the woodworking, the bushcraft, the woodland management work I do, is about creating opportunities for people to practically work with their hands with the stuff that comes out of woodlands or the local landscape where they live. And that literally connects them to the landscape, and that's why it's such an interesting magical project.

I asked Greg to expand on this idea and the role of magic in his artwork.

I think the first thing we have to agree on is that artwork does not have to be defined by an object that is created. For me the object is just the end part of the art process. Occasionally people ask me to create objects for them; as well as garden lines, dibbers and wattle hurdles these could also be rune sets, wands, staffs etc, but for me this sort of misses the point. I would much rather take them into the woods and teach them to make their own object. Saying that, I do undertake one-off commissions if people cannot practically make their own, and in these cases I supply the object and a handmade record (through sketches etc) of the process of production.

The courses I run, and the woodland management work I do, can involve coppicing, bushcraft, green woodwork or traditional archery; but through this outdoor process-based practice a bond is created during creation between the maker/landowner and the geographical place where the material was gathered and the object created. Each object, whether it is coppiced woodland, a cup, a rune set, an arrow, a walking stick or a chair becomes a touchstone reminding that person of the place where it came from and their memory of it. It builds the energetic connection, like a rainbow bridge, between the maker and the place. That patch of woodland begins to grow within their inner landscape and through the imagination they are forever connected to that place. They can travel there astrally whenever they want to and tap into the feelings of relaxation, peace, freedom, resourcefulness, perseverance, pride in their own abilities, or whatever feelings arose when they spent time creating the object/touchstone in the woods. That's the true gift, that's the magick.

Ultimately, I hope that the people who come and work with me, whether they want to make a magical object, are making traditional bows or learning to make fire using a bow drill will have a deeper and enriched relationship with nature. They get to see the land as an entity, a living growing being. They can also see how nature is useful, it provides us with everything we need to live on this planet in a comfortable and healthy way and this is one of the important points in terms of my art.

Coppice timber pile on woodland managed by Greg

This deep transformational process is important to Greg as an example of 'The King' a term derived from the later work of Thee Temple Ov Psychick Youth.

I see this idea of the King as "the invocation and manifestation of the Being that wants the best for all Beings; and has the ability to manifest this". For me, I see this process as the unfolding of the Knowledge and Conversation of the Holy Guardian Angel, and on a personal level it's the result of the work we did in NTWICCM Volumes 1–3 (note—Volume 3 was actually a ritual process rather than a printed text). It's a very humbling idea as it places the believer in a position where they come to understand they themselves do not have the capacity to bring this about and ask for aid. I don't have a clear idea of what the result is going to be of this invocation. As a magician, to invoke a being is to call something in. It's a request for help. For that being to come in and do its work you need to move out of the way. Surrender, and let it take over. That means in chaos magick terms the intention of the work is not results based.

The idea has resonances with Blake's Jerusalem for me. The hope and faith that all will be well, where a harmonious future for all beings is possible and beautiful beyond our imaginations. Where we all are strong, happy and healthy and connected to the place where we live, to the green and pleasant land, the pure air, the clean water, the warm sun, with love in all our hearts. Now, obviously this is a romanticized Utopian future philosophy, but the idea of the King is that if you are going to believe something, then believe something beautiful! And if you truly believe that magick can change the world, then do it for the best result you could not even imagine! After all, with magick, anything is possible.

Can you explain more about your experiences with ayahuasca?

I think for magick to work it requires a change in consciousness and there are many ways of achieving this; meditation, dancing, drumming, yoga, etc, but for me psychoactive plants and their derivatives have held a particular fascination. They have changed the way I see the world, they have altered my consciousness. When the opportunity in the late 1990s came for me to meet this exotic and mysterious medicine from the Amazon called ayahuasca I jumped at the chance. What appealed to me was the ritual use of these psychoactive plants coming from a culture where they had been in continuous ritual use for thousands of years. The practice and knowledge of how to work with these plants has been refined by practitioners for all that span of time. I actually knew very little about it at the time and there weren't that many Western Europeans who had experience of it, but through some Brazilian friends I came into contact with the Church of Santo Daime.

The Church of Santo Daime is an ayahuasca church with many adherents throughout the world. The Church grew from the Amazon, through non-indigenous people working in the forest coming into contact with indigenous people. When these caboclos, and descendants of emancipated African slaves, went to look for healing with the local tribespeople they were given ayahuasca. From these experiences, and with their teachers' consent, people such as Raimundo Irineu Serra took the medicine from the forest to the towns and cities of Brazil. On its journey ayahusaca formed a syncretic belief system [around itself] in order to introduce the medicine to non-indigenous people. The belief system is a mix of indigenous shamanism, Catholicism, and African nature worship called Umbanda; but really it is a fluid belief system which grows and changes organically with the beliefs of the participants. There is now an Eastern current appearing in many ayahuasca ceremonies where many of the songs include bhajans and chants from India. It seemed the perfect platform for me, coming from a chaos magick background with its core tenet of "all beliefs are equally valid".

Now, before I start talking about my experience with ayahuasca, I feel the need to discuss generally the way I have perceived the medicine to work. For many drinkers of ayahuasca there is a common experience of exploring the inner workings of the soul. This can initially be blissful, but at some stage also includes exploring the darker, hidden areas of ourselves which we normally don't want to see. With these plant medicines (ayahuasca, peyote, San Pedro) there is no escape from this experience; and in the Santo Daime Church it is called the Passagem (or "the passage"), and it can be profoundly uncomfortable. I feel the difference between these medicines and 'drugs' is that there is a narrative to this plant medicine experience, and the real work for the participant is learning from this journey and successfully applying it in their own life. If they can do that, I believe it can deliver true transformation of themselves and the world around them.

Most long-term participants understand the objective experience of this journey, but the subjective experience is completely different for each person depending on many factors including; who they are, where they come from, family history etc. This experience commonly takes the form of visions and physical sensation. In the visions, beings or entities often appear and they seem to have a separate, autonomous agenda to your own. By that I mean you have little or no control over them. (A common encounter with these beings begins with them asking, "What are you doing here?"). To all intents and purposes they are independent entities and even though we could explain that experience in psychotherapeutic language (metaphor, archetypes etc.), that does not really convey the experience very satisfactorily, so I prefer to use the language of shamanism (spirits, beings etc.) as I feel it does a better job. So please, when I talk of my own experience with these medicines it is important to understand this is my own journey, and if anyone has the opportunity to meet ayahuasca then their journey will be a very different one. However, I feel it's worth relating my story as it highlights some sense of the experience, and also how it has shaped my artistic and magickal practice.

Before my meeting with ayahuasca I suppose I was expecting an experience similar to psilocybin, or LSD. In the first few sessions I was transported in vision to a beautiful, purple and pink forest, dripping with rain and full of life. These were visions where I could see, touch, smell, taste and hear the forest in full 3D. To all intents and purposes I was transported there. However, after the second or third session things changed.

I found myself in a white room, the floor covered with sand. A condor sat on the sand and immediately buried itself until it couldn't be seen, and in the corner of the room I could see a black cat.

"Aaah, cute", I said to myself, "The cat looks a bit like Sylvester from the Tweetie Pie cartoons".

At which point the cat jumped at me, baring huge, sharp teeth and bit me, tearing me apart. I couldn't stand up in the hall where my body was, and I had to lie down at the rear of the room, vomiting copiously. The pain was incredible and seemed to be all encompassing. It was as if I was drowning in it, and couldn't find a way out. I had a back injury from a snowboarding accident several years earlier and this became the epicentre of the pain.

0   1

Metamorphosis   Yetsirah

From The Daime Colouring Book

This continued for about a year. I would take ayahuasca regularly and each time the Jaguar (for that is how the Cat manifested) would come unbidden. I would try everything I could think of to control it; fighting, summoning spirits to help me, running away, casting protective circles, hiding... everything a powerful chaos magician could conjure. All to no avail. The Jaguar would catch me and rip me apart every time, I would be in utter agony and lie down vomiting. There was no escape. I learnt many things about myself in this period, my controlling nature, my capacity for violence, anger and fear.

After about a year of this I couldn't take any more. I resolved to return one last time to meet the Jaguar, and if I couldn't work it out then I would have to stop drinking ayahuasca. It seemed too much like returning to be abused. Even though I felt better after each session, it was too much. Too hard, too painful to keep going back for more.

The Jaguar came as it always did. It approached me and I held up my hands.

"Whoa, whoa", I said, "Please, stop. I don't know what to do to stop you from hurting me. I have done everything I can think of and none of it works. Please help me, please tell me what I need to do to stop you hurting me. I surrender."

At which point the jaguar opened its mouth again and I braced myself for another attack; but it never came. The Jaguar's mouth stretched wider and wider until it became a pink lined tunnel descending very deep. I entered the tunnel and it led me to a beautiful garden carpeted with flowers and full of butterflies, bees and hummingbirds. All the pain had gone leaving me with a feeling of ecstatic bliss, open hearted and full of light. The demon had turned into an angel, transporting me to another world. Amazing!

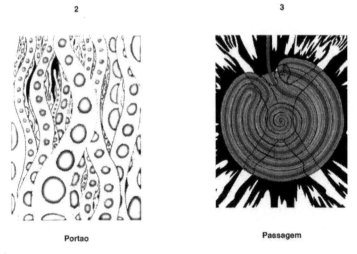

2   3

Portao   Passagem

From The Daime Colouring Book

I felt released from a prison, free to move, and from that day I have not had any trouble from my back injury. Somehow the process had healed it and given me a revelation regarding the process of healing with these plant medicines. It showed me that physical injuries have an emotional component and an energetic component; and that to heal them we can work on any of these levels (Reiki, massage, Western Medicine, acupuncture etc) but the plant medicines add an extra level to this. The visions allow us to access a mythical, metaphorical, spiritual, symbolic component of ourselves, and if we can resolve the relationship between ourselves and the beings that appear to us at this level, then the healing reverberates through the other levels, transforming the pain into light.

For me this was a massively humbling experience that also transformed my magickal practice. The Jaguar led me on a path that subjugated my Will, to the Will of a Higher Being. I could no longer perform magickal operations purely for "My Will" any more. I had to get out of the way to a certain extent in order to leave space to allow that other Being in, and let it do its Will. The jaguar made me realise I needed to surrender to the idea that I could not do this alone, and that I was no longer the most important being in the Universe. In short magick became an "art" in the best sense of the word, using a change in consciousness to transform myself and the world around me. Of course, inherent in the very idea I can change the world there is ego and a certain amount of dancing between My Will and Higher Will; but it is an art that arises from an altruistic desire to create things of beauty for the world. Not just for me, but for everybody else as well. In fact, not just the people on this planet, but all the beings and spirits that occupy this space. Magick is the process by which consciousness can alter objective reality, and plant medicines are the tool I often choose to achieve that.

For me, the Jaguar Story illustrates a really important point about magickal practice that often gets ignored. Many of the magicians I have met seem incredibly courageous and adept at dealing with the shadows, the dark and scary parts of themselves (and life in general) but they seem to get trapped inside that, and find it incredibly difficult stepping into the Light. Releasing control, and surrendering to the beauty of their soul, opening their hearts seems much harder. The Mayan tradition tells of a God called Tezcatlipoca who holds two mirrors; one is a smoky black obsidian mirror that shows you all the dark, shadowy parts of yourself and the other is a bright, shining mirror that shows all the amazing beauty you are. For me, the ability and skill of the adept magician is to look simultaneously into both mirrors and to move effortlessly between them, between the worlds. Magick doesn't have to always be dark and hidden, and to function successfully and happily in the objective universe I have found it most effective to be nice to people, kind, generous, giving, and loving as much as I can, to keep smiling, to enjoy myself and laugh a lot.

Greg helping students from University College Falmouth to create a living willow structure.

I wonder how does Greg see his work as a magician, an artist and woodsman developing?

What does the future hold? There are an increasing number of possible futures for us I feel. The internet and the increasing speed of communication make more and more possible all the time. Whatever happens though, I feel the most important thing for us to remember is our reliance on, and connection with Nature. Technology is all well and good, and I am no Luddite—the internet is probably the most important invention in the history of the human race; but if we don't have clean drinking water—we die; if we don't have healthy food to eat— we die, if we don't have clean air to breathe—we die; and if we don't have shelter against the extremes of weather and a sustainable source of heat—we die. There is a danger that the increasing reliance on technology disassociates us from these basic facts of life on this planet. There was a philosopher called Albert Borgmann back in the day and he wrote a series of essays called The Uses of Technology *where he foresaw this distancing from nature and urged people to re-align themselves with these primary needs.*

Now, I know this sounds like a huge marketing pitch for the courses I run [laughs] but I really do believe that the essentials of the ability for us to survive on this world should be taught to everyone, and at the core of that is Fire, Food, Shelter and Water. If people do not have the ability to get these things for themselves they will be bound to a structure or system to supply them. Fear and Stockhausen Syndrome will be a constant companion in that case where people are reliant on increasingly unstable governmental structures to provide the basics of life. It's not that I advocate a return to some hunter-gatherer existence, or expect everyone to chop wood to build a fire on a daily basis, but more that we understand the importance of these things and have the ability *to do them if needed. Just knowing we have the ability to get the essentials of life for ourselves, from Nature, releases us from a baseline anxiety, or fear, that if we lose our jobs we will not be able to provide the things we and our loved ones need and—in extremis—we will die.*

In a sense my artistic practice deals with these essentials of life, necessary for us to exist on this world, and therefore they remain a constant (unless we evolve into a cyborg race or something) so the changes happening with technology don't really affect that. On a magickal or esoteric level I deal with the Old Gods, running in the wind, or tunnelling in the ground; plant and Nature spirits connected to each other and us through this common bond of life on this blue jewel floating in an ink black sea. The New Gods of Internet and Technology are interesting, but I leave them to others to elevate and exalt; the Old Gods underpin everything and without them we won't be here to make the new ones.

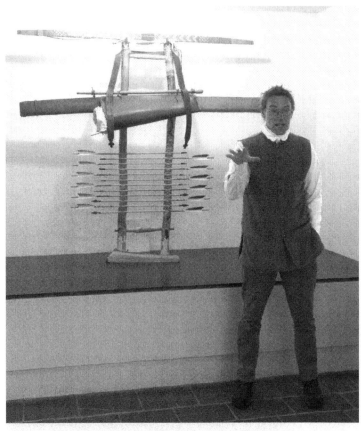

Greg presenting The Bow of Albion
at the Penwith Gallery, St Ives 2018.
(Photograph courtesy of Amanda Richardson.)

Children in the Circle:
Paganism, Spirituality and our Families

The role of families and children in contemporary Paganism.

Hanging up decorations to celebrate Yule, carving pumpkins at Halloween, dancing round the Maypole and more—these are at once modern Pagan activities, folk customs and stuff that kids can get involved with. Those of us who have the honour and delight to be parents get to engage in some very interesting questions when it comes to the relationship between our own spiritual practices and our kids.

What is the context for what's going on? In a significantly secular culture such Britain (around 25% of English citizens describe their religion as 'none') there is a tendency to think that spirituality (or the apparent lack of it) is down to personal choice and conscience. Britain is also a spiritually diverse landscape and the place of origin of a number of new religious movements.

It's also true that the social function of religion in Britain is somewhat different from that of, say, the USA. With these considerations in mind how do we, as families, integrate our own spirituality with raising children?

Hanging up the Yule/Christmas/Mithrasmas/Winterval decorations is a good example. This is an embodied practice, one that we can give multiple meanings to. A ritual like this can be something children can enjoy and participate in. In my household I describe what we're doing in, what I hope, is a very open-ended way: 'We're making the house look fun because it's dark and we're going to have a few days of holiday where we can watch movies, eat nice food, and snuggle by the open fire. We are celebrating the fact of the longest night, the beginning of the New Year, and the slow return of the light'. My approach is, I hope, broad enough that they can appreciate what we did in Pagan, Humanist, Atheist, Christian or other terms. They also don't have to join in. I'm totally happy to put the tree up and install the ivy myself though I find that naturally, they want to help.

There are many aspects of my own spiritual life from which my children are excluded. All of the esoteric groups I work with maintain policies that preclude the admission of anyone under the age of at least 18 (the intensity and intimacy of group magical practice is a space that demands an adult maturity). In other cultures, these things differ. Children are most certainly present at ceremonies such as the Healing Dance of the San people from South Africa. In this rite dancing and singing continues long into the night as people are possessed by spirits (an event, which in that culture, is attended by bleeding through the nose). Mothers sit on the sand with their babies and, at least before they get tired and bored, the younger San kids run around the outside of the ritual space, pretending to get possessed and generally making fun of the shamans in the circle, mimicking their hunched over dancing postures and dripping noses. Just as one might expect.

One of the benefits of my Pagan spirituality is that it allows me to include my children in public and gentle ceremonies of celebration (such as the ones that take place at St Nectan's Glen in Cornwall and at many other sacred sites in the British Isles), as well as our own domestic traditions. Because these traditions are rooted in the flow of the seasons they are open to interpretation and elaboration in many different ways. Intelligent children (and of course my kids are really bright) readily understand this. My eldest son, many years ago, pointed out that the sun coming back from the solstice at Yule was paralleled by the resurrection of the mythic lion Aslan in *The Lion, the Witch and the Wardrobe*. And that this was basically the same as the story of Osiris and also Jesus. Personally I tend to avoid names of deities (though we all have a soft spot for Ganesh, and through the medium of Marvel comics both my kids are getting more interested in Norse mythology). Instead we talk about what we're doing as people connected to the landscape we're in. It's all about relationships and perspectives. At the Equinox I explain that this time is about noticing that light and dark are equal, and realising that this is one of only two days in the year where the day and night length is pretty much equal all across the whole world. No deities, no rules, no dogma, just a scientific fact that we're choosing to notice and celebrate.

As well as including our children in accessible and culturally appropriate aspects of our spirituality we can also learn from them. For Lammas this year, at the suggestion of my eldest son, we made special biscuits to celebrate the fact that the harvest had come. This has become something of a theme (I mean homemade biscuits! What's not to like?). My children made two batches of biscuits that we shared with participants at a public Pagan ritual we attended. Chocolate ones for the dark of the year, and banana and vanilla ones for the light. In this way, my kids are building for themselves a family and community tradition. I only hope that they don't follow through on some of the more grotesque suggestions they seem to be considering for their Halloween recipe!

Cookies of light and of darkness

Inspiration from the Darkness:
The Psychology of Magick

An exploration of the relationship between psychology and 'real' magic.

Here's a description of a ritual that I did with Steve Dee and Nikki Wyrd. The aim of this practice was to enter the darkness of the coming year, and be nourished by that time in order to empower the writing work that we're all engaged in at the moment. This is particularly helpful for me as, like many folks who live here in Britain, I sometimes find the darkness of the year psychologically challenging.

For some people this kind of magic looks perilously close to psychology. I've certainly seen folks getting exercised about how their gods are not 'just archetypes' and their mystical path is something much more profound than neurological hacking plus a pointy hat. In my view this kind of opinion perhaps misses the point that psychology is simply the study of the mind. I'm not sure that there is anything much more magical than the psyche and, moreover, given that all magical acts (even those with apparently measurable parapsychological effects) require a mind somewhere in their operation, the working knowledge of said psyche may well add to the efficacy of any magical operation.

There is also the confusing idea of 'real'. Magician and writer Nick Farrell addresses in a blog article what he sees as the overly psychological approach to magic; "Personally I would like an NLP 'expert' to try to explain a real Daemon as an extension of their unconscious as it strangles him or her with his own intestines." The problem with 'reality' is that it is inevitably mediated through inter-subjective consensus (i.e. people's minds). But anyone with an appreciation of psychology will appreciate that the mind is also 'real'. Placebos, psychosomatic illnesses and the power of positive thinking are all real, and indeed have hard-science measurable effects. Whether a demon (however arcane our choice of spelling) can, in a literal measurable sense, strangle someone using their own gut is, I would suggest, open to debate (and a request for proof).

Those familiar with the four models of magic proposed by Frater U∴D∴ will also recognise that the 'psychological paradigm', rather than being a species of 'magic lite' is actually just one way of describing what is going on. Given that it is currently the dominant model in our culture (most people 'believe in' psychology whereas explicit belief in occult energies or demons is perhaps less common), it is no less useful (or true) than the energy, spirit or information models. There is also a lot of very useful research that has emerged from psychology (in its many forms, from transpersonal psychology to sociology, psychoneurology and more) and the wise magician is likely to find much of value in the grimoires of those disciplines.

And so, to Work!

In robes we descend to my subterranean temple space. Here under the earth we have prepared candles, a strobe light, smoke machine, incense and suitable chthonic sounding music. We begin by holding hands (because that's always nice). We take four breaths together; one for the sky above us, one for the earth within which we sit, one for the water that surrounds our island of Britain, and one for the fire in our hearts.

I strike the singing bowl and read the invocation of Baphomet (from *The Book of Baphomet*).

We sit for a while in silence.

Still seated in the circle we begin playing drums, manjïrà, blowing a conch, striking singing bowls and using our voices. The music is loud, the strobe machine flashes bright pulsing light in the underground chamber. As the smoke swirls around us we contact the darkness, the earth, bringing our attention to the fact that winter is coming.

The music ends and we go upstairs, into the light and the brightness. We light incense and more candles. An image of Thoth, god of writing, graces the altar. We begin by shaking our bodies, loosening up and then dance to some suitably uplifting music.

Finally, we laugh and embrace; the ritual ends.

This basic technique; a movement from dark to light was done on the day of the September equinox. Our rite is both a celebration of this time and a way of orienting ourselves to the coming experience. We could have dressed it up with more bells and smells, more favourite deities and even demonic seals and other elaborate ceremonialism. We could have added mind-expanding substances or barbaric languages but sometimes magic can just be simple. As simple as psychology, but no less magical for all that.

Taw river spirits in September

On Being a Priest

The exoteric expression of esoteric practice as ministry.

While some aspects of esoteric endeavour can be highly personal and private, there are other expressions of it that are profoundly relevant to other people, including those who aren't necessarily into all that other spooky occult stuff. The work of the celebrant or priest(ess) is one such example of this.

Over the years I've been asked to perform numerous handfastings, namings, house blessings and, at time of writing, one requiem. Many of my magical colleagues have also performed rites of this type. Sometimes we are asked by people who identify as pagans, while on other occasions the request come from 'friends of friends'; from people who want a ceremony that sits outside of the Anglican Christian framework which remains the default style for rites of passage among many folk in the British Isles (though in a greatly attenuated form).

The work of the celebrant provides some measure of the significant social role played by shamans in indigenous cultures. While it's not easy (or respectful or ethnographically accurate...) to generalise about shamanism, it is perhaps fair to suggest that the shaman's activity has a recognized social role. In contrast the trappings of Western occulture; magic circles, demonic seals, mystical titles and the rest—to many non-occultists, looks little different from slightly-bonkers live action role play. However, when asked by our (Western) community to help provide rites of passage, we are performing the social role played by esoteric specialists (be they shamans, priests or others) in other cultures both past and present.

Creating a good ritual is important. I was asked to provide a marriage ceremony for two friends who were getting wed on the island of Sicily. The rite I created—in close consultation with the happy couple—had to make sense and be emotionally moving for them, plus ten British guests, and forty Sicilians from the bride's family. Fortunately, the neo-pagan canon and my own experience meant that I was able to hold the space successfully and create an experience which uplifted everyone there. Simple, almost universally understood acts—exchanging rings, asking people to give a blessing and offer a candle to the couple, constructing a circle of flowers within which they stand, consecrating their union with earth, with water, air and fire as they held hands, and finally they kiss. This is the language of simple ritual, handily getting around the need for too much translation for either English or Italian speakers. People cried—in a good way—and one chap (who actually turned out to be a member of the Carabinieri) was really taken with the whole thing ('magificane, bello, spirituale!'), which was nice.

The blessing of air, Sicilian style

As with much group ritual, creating a good handfasting or other ceremony is often a collaborative work. It's important to be able to listen to the needs of the people involved as much as coming with one's own preconceptions about how things 'should' be done. It's also important to be able to adapt to local circumstances.

At a recent wedding that Nikki Wyrd and I did in North Wales, we wanted to incorporate the 'traditional' jumping over the broomstick. Rather than do this at the ceremony itself we waited until the morning after (the main rite took place by the sea and carrying a broom down the scramble to the isolated cove we were using wouldn't have been easy); moreover the dramatic reveal of the broom itself would have been spoiled. Given the style of the people we were acting as celebrants to, rather than a classic besom we instead bound ribbons around their own yard brush, combining the magical and mundane in a way we judged would both amuse and move them.

Jumping into a new life, together!
(Photograph courtesy of Graeme Hartley-Martin)

The practice of facilitating rites of passage also helps the individual magician maintain an outward focus for their work, and not disappear up their own ouroboros, into an introspective haze of rarefied magic-isms. Doing social ritual means understanding how people work, what is likely to move them, what ritual techniques can be successful in different settings, and being able to hold the space in a way that privileges the experience of those undertaking the ritual rather than the authority of the magician themselves.

As I've written before: if we work with spirits, the most important spirits we meet on a daily basis are other humans. Finding good ways to be with these spirits, especially when we are entrusted to help them in rites of passage, is for me a great honour. Being asked to do this kind of work is also a confirmation of my status in the minds of others. Not as some super powerful magician (or whatever) but as someone who can blend the authority and skill necessary to hold ritual space with the sensitivity required to respond to the needs of others.

The test for whether one is actually a shaman or a priest is not how we like to style ourselves, but how others refer to us. And while one might be mindful of the sort of ego inflation such titles may engender there is also the need to honestly face the truth. That the magic I do does have a value and relevance in my wider community, and so I am grateful to the universe that I can perform this Great Work for the benefit of others.

Psychedelic Ceremony in Theory and Practice

A presentation I gave at the conference on psychedelic consciousness Breaking Convention at the University of Greenwich 2017.

I'm going to talk about in this presentation about psychedelic ceremony. I'm going to give a range of examples of these practices and finish by considering the opportunities and challenges that face us, the growing, planet wide, psychedelic community.

I suspect we the people at this conference have a broadly shared consensus of what we mean by 'psychedelic'. Our consensus would probably be around ideas like altered or extraordinary states of consciousness. The 'conscious' bit matters; these are states of awareness, things we can recall, however imperfectly, when back in what we describe as our baseline or 'normal' states of awareness. The 'extraordinary' component of our definition reflects our subjective perception that these states are ones that are different, sometimes radically different, from the states of awareness that we usually in. To use one of the latest descriptions for what the psychedelic state is; we can describe it as one in which the connectivity across brain regions is significantly changed (or perhaps more accurately 'normal' cognition is down regulated and other connections emerge). We know that these mind states can be induced through a wide variety of practices; sex, dance, meditation, protracted periods of darkness, breathwork and of course by introducing various substances into our bodies.

But what is ceremony? When we think of ritual and ceremony we may imagine military or civic rites. Those of formal religious or public occasions. Celebrations of a particular event, achievement, or anniversary. We may imagine that words like 'ritual' or 'ceremony' indicate a series of actions performed according to a prescribed order. We might imagine a 'solemn act, formal and dignified, characterized by deep sincerity'. Equally we might imagine the wild bacchanalia or carnival. Ritual and ceremony is a broad church but in the sense that I using it here I'm interested in ceremony as *the intentional use of metaphor to affect the imaginal world.*

Ceremony for me is a natural activity for symbol using, meaning making creatures such as ourselves. Sure sometimes it may be formal in nature; at other times it may well up as a spontaneous gesture. Laying flowers at the site of a tragic event, wrapping presents, ritually disposing of our dead. These are things our species does. Ceremony then is the deployment of acts that are symbolic, frequently metaphorical, sometimes carefully planned, sometimes free-form and spontaneously arising in the moment.

In context of the use of psychedelic drugs, psychedelic ceremony is the manipulation of sets and settings within which we might explore those remarkably potent and remarkably safe experiences offered by medicines such as DMT, ayahuasca, mescaline, LSD and all those other fascinating chemicals, the power and significance of which we are celebrating and exploring at this conference.

Why not 'psychedelic session'? Why use the religious sounding word 'ceremony?' Well there are two reasons for this:

The first is that I come to psychedelics as an occultist, an indigenous 'shaman' of the British Isles, and so I tend to think in those terms. Occultism is the study of that which is hidden, such as the relationship between matter and mind, a relationship that psychedelic drugs bring into stark relief. The practice by which this exploration happens is usually called 'magic' which we could think of as *the use of the imaginal world to extend the limits of our achievable reality.*

The second and bigger reason is that the sense of the sacred that these substances can generate I feel demands the use of a word that goes beyond the apparently 'secular' expressions 'session' or 'experiment'. The word 'ceremony' itself derives from a Latin root that suggests ideals of holiness, sacredness and awe. Sure many people eschew anything that sounds 'religious' but I feel that using this word shows both respect to those indigenous traditions who use entheogens, and reclaims the word from the dead hand of doctrinal belief. We need not throw the baby of the sacred out with the bathwater of religious dogma.

Looked at through the lens of contemporary neurology we could say that this sense of the divine is what we experience when the psychedelicized brain lights like a Christmas tree in an fMRI scanner. Considered in a historical sense we can see how psychedelic substances are often implicated in the genesis of religions; the blue-throated mushroom of Shiva, the burning acacia of Moses, the kykeon of Eleusis. The pharmacological reality and subjective numinosity of these experiences need not be incommensurate with each other.

We are fortunate to be living in a time when knowledge about methods to hold, support and direct the psychedelic state is increasingly abundant. Today there is a great confluence of wisdom from 'traditional' practitioners, underground psychonauts and licensed scientific researchers. In the West, since the time of Tim Leary et al., we have known that the mental state and the environment can profoundly influence the way that our drug trip unfolds. Western culture itself has created ceremonial settings in response to the emergence of two widely available psychedelic drugs. Our first attempt at this was the creation of the music festival, our culture's collective response to LSD. Later we created the rave to hold the experience of MDMA. Our indigenous shamanic intelligence gave rise to the First and Second Summers of Love.

Psychedelic drugs are special, powerful things that by their very nature stimulate a feeling of 'the sacred' and this feeling runs deep. This feeling often inspires people not only to create specific environments, and ceremonies for their psychedelic sessions, but also during the process of producing the drugs in the first place.

Whether we are mindfully rolling a joint, or singing as we stir the bubbling pot of ayahuasca, the preparation of these medicines evokes a sense of the sacred. It becomes a ceremony.

There is, for example, some fascinating research to be done on the use of ceremony by contemporary clandestine chemists. I spoke with former psychedelic chemist Casey Hardison and asked whether he did anything he would consider to be a 'ceremony' when he produced, for instance, LSD. Casey told me that he used crystals, smudging with sage and other practices during some of this work. He had a practice of setting LSD to crystalize while music played; 'Righteous Rasta music' structured to echo the pattern of the chakras in Asian esoteric anatomy. Asked why, Casey said that his intention was that the molecule would somehow be affected by the music, helping those who took the drug to "absorb the energy of loving themselves, allowing them to have the highest vibrational experience".

Casey was by no means unique in his practice. To quote Cosmo Feilding Mellen in an interview about the film he directed The Sunshine Makers:

> The purity of different types of acids was an important part of psychedelic culture. People believed that the purer the acid, the better the trip. It was all very subjective, of course—Owsley would pay attention to the music they were playing in the lab at the point of crystallisation, and would then pray over the equipment to imbue it with positive vibes. Tim (Scully) was a rational scientist and initially thought it was all mumbo jumbo, but he eventually got sucked into it.

The unfortunately still incarcerated LSD chemist William Leonard Pickard mentions the ritualization of psychedelic synthesis in his wonderful book *The Rose of Paracelsus*. In a recent email to me he wrote:

> Indigo [an LSD chemist] mentions Gregorian chant during synthesis or crystallization, often Amazonian shamanic, soft, gentle chanting. From my interviews of very high-level manufacturers in the 80's–90's for drug policy research, I recall most fondly one individual [who] never dream of conducting a crystallization without Vivaldi's 'The Four Seasons' playing in one continuous loop, quite loud, for

many hours from start to finish. He did so for years. Something about the beauty of the molecules finding each other, and the harmony of the seasons. The Vivaldi seems to be a lineage in certain groups.

In all these examples—leaving aside any parapsychological or subtle physical interpretations of what may or may not happen when one crystallizes LSD in the presence of music—what we can see is that these chemists are doing ceremony. They are creating a set of poetic, metaphorical relationships to influence their set by changing their setting (putting on certain music). They are doing so while in a psychedelically altered state (laboratory spillages, as even extremely thorough Swiss chemists know very well, can and do happen). They are using this poetic language of behaviour with a specific intention—that of making the best LSD; to make good medicine.

Let's break down the idea of psychedelic ceremony in a little more detail and give a few examples of practices.

When we drink alcohol we say 'cheers'! We make an invocation to the spirit of happiness, perhaps a toast of greater or lesser complexity. So too in many traditions and approaches to psychedelics will people take a moment before they take the drug. That pregnant pause we have, sat before the awesome reality of the loaded DMT pipe. Some like to say a prayer over their drugs, some do this by offering their lover a pill in their mouth, ending the kiss with the words 'have a good one'.

Depending on the nature of the psychedelic adventure, the location where the experience will unfold may have been specially prepared. The style may be very varied. From complex patterned fabrics and ready-to-undulate-when-the-mushrooms -kick-in wooden flooring, through to white walls and soft cushions. The point about the space is that it supports and directs the experience and therefore, in whatever way we choose, it demands our attention.

Re-set your Set by sorting out your Setting. As we clean the room, and place our power objects around us; pictures of our family perhaps, or of deities, of sports cars or kittens (if that's our thing) we develop a deep sense that all is well. The mutual relationship of Set and Setting means any act of preparation (which could instead be about getting all glammed up if we are going out clubbing) is an instinctive ceremonial process.

Some locations look very clearly like psychedelic ceremonial space. The beautiful crescent altar of the peyote circle, marked with the long glorious road that the participants take through the night together. Other ritual spaces may have a more modern look, with specially selected images projected upon the walls, sigils glowing in the blacklight and rotating dream machines. As psychonauts we make these psychedelic autonomous zones, these ceremonial spaces, in many ways. From spontaneously arising moments when we realise and respond to the sacred, through more formal group rituals, to gatherings so large we call them festivals.

There are many groups in many countries that meet to do these kinds of ceremonies; some are peer-led, others with more formal structures, often inspired by indigenous entheogenic cultures of the Americas or elsewhere. For some people their psychedelic ceremonies are solitary affairs, perhaps lone psychogeographical wanderings or night long solitary vigils, still others make pilgrimage to the temples wh ere God is a DJ.

Once we are tripping we can use our skills to make the best use of our time in that space however it is constructed. While sometimes all we need is to lie down and let the experience take us, at other points we may like to do stuff; anything from contemplating the aeons old architecture of our own hands, through to creative practices such as making art or singing and dancing.

As the psychedelic state is so plastic we can make interventions here; in some contexts we might think of these as acts of psychological neurohacking, or perhaps sorcery, in any case they are examples of deploying symbolic activity with an intention.

For example. We can use mimetic magic also known as sympathetic magic. We create a psychological link; *as X happens so Y follows*, 'magical thinking' or perhaps 'thinking magically'. This works especially well when we are high and different (novel) parts of our minds are connected. The embodied psychedelic experience recalls the magicians' axiom 'as above so below, as within so without'. In psychedelic ceremony we are deploying symbolic action within the interrelated network of all things which, when not high, we experience as discrete objects.

Let's take a not too woo-woo psychological example of how this works: We might for example become aware that, when difficult memories of a failed relationship arise during the trip, that we screw our face up and hunch our shoulders. In the psychedelic state, where everything in the mind (and who knows, perhaps all things in the universe) is connected, we make a magical link; 'as I relax my tense muscles so I find a way to sit in equanimity with the pain of my past'. As we relax, passing through the journey of that intention, our state of mind while tripping, and our subsequent relationships with others after we come down, also relaxes and becomes easier.

Then there can be things that look more like spells in the proper witchcraft-pointy-hat sense. One might do a spell to encourage the conditions in society in which the benefits of psychedelic drugs can be widely appreciated. This spell could aim to find ourselves in a better relationship, as a species, with these divine medicines. One might do this by creating a magical sculpture, a physical form for a spirit, giving it a name and celebrating it as a god. Offering our psychedelic gnosis to it, desiring that it is empowered to carry this intention into the complex web of Wyrd that connects all things. You can see what we in magic call the 'material base' of such a spell, cast from within psychedelic ceremony, in the museum here at Breaking Convention.

*IZAWA Spirit of the Liberation of the Psychedelic Gnosis.
On display in The Psychedelic Museum gallery at Breaking
Convention 2017.*

Let's consider another ceremony which can be deployed very easily by the psychonaut. We can think of this as a handy neurohack:

We know that our bodies primarily get our conscious attention when things go wrong. We experience the alert of pain and discomfort when there is a problem. Most of the time we don't notice our left foot unless it hurts.

We also know that cultivating an optimistic and grateful attitude has benefits on everything from the functionality of our own immune systems to our broader mental health, and that this well-being thereby affects others. It's a particularly powerful charm against depression, both individually and culturally.

(Technically this is left-hand path vajrayana, fourth turning of the wheel of dharma teaching we're talking here; check it out if you've not already grokked that stuff).

To cultivate this beneficial attitude we take a moment to thank all those things that are good. To deliberately take our attention away from the painful and the incessant human desire to solve whatever currently is 'the problem'. One way of by doing this is by smoking in a ceremonial style.

Let's set the scene for this easy-to-do psychedelic ceremony: I walk away from the bonfire and the pumping sound system. I've got a pre-rolled joint or tobacco smoke in hand. I kneel down on the dry grass. I am here to pray. I ceremonially breathe the smoke of the joint up to the sky, then directly down onto the earth, I then blow it to the left and right and finally towards the moon above me. This metaphorical ritual process orientates me within the world. I use the joint to focus me in the moment and I pray, speaking about what I love, counting my blessings. There are many imagined locations to which we might address our prayer. Simply to 'The Universe', or for the those more theologically inclined 'the Great Goddess'. Personally I rather like 'Great Spirit' or 'Great Mystery', and sometimes 'Baphomet'. We may silently formulate our prayer or it speak aloud. Aloud is good since it permits our spontaneous, heart-felt words to travel out into our surroundings. Their reverberations fall back into our own ears, forming a new neural pathway. In our prayers we remember all those things we are grateful for; those who love us, our health, this life, these medicines, the cool of the night air. Whatever we really love and what fills us with joy and we take delight in.

When I'm done I bury the end of the joint in the earth, nod my thanks to the moon and return to the pumping sound of the party...

Our psychedelic ceremony, however we do it, unfolds...

Perhaps, towards the tail end of the trip, you decide to do some divination by consulting the tarot, using those strange occult images to explore the relationships of things in your life that are important. Changing your perspective and looking on the problem as though from the outside, finding new possibilities. You can do something similar through the process that psychologists call a 'sculpt', using found or specially selected objects to represent characters or situations. Just as the psychedelic state joins up bits of our brain, so we can express and reflect internal processes through external symbol sets, in order to discover novel interpretations and gain new understanding and capacity to change things.

These techniques of divination can be usefully employed when we are high: from ones where a meaning is sought in what some claim is random stuff, such the shapes of clouds, or of fire, or the first three runes picked from a bag. By interpreting these symbols, and perhaps manipulating them in some way, we open ourselves to new possibilities. It's also the case that, in my experience, what parapsychologists call 'hits' happen more commonly when we are in an altered state of awareness.

Whether simple or highly structured, lasting just half an hour or several days, eventually our psychedelic ceremony comes to an end.

As the dawn breaks we sweep clear the circle around the crescent altar and place the final sticks with impeccable care on the arrow fire. We tidy up after the party. We thank the spirits or the power of the time, the place, the medicine. We allow ourselves time to come down, to enjoy the shamanic return to a world renewed and full of possibility. To reflect, to eat, to sleep, to dream.

And, each of us a shaman, we bring back the insights from that trip into the psychedelic ultraworld for the benefit of ourselves and community.

What insights might we gather from these psychedelic adventures? Too many to list of course, but considering the value of these substances in themselves, what might be learnt?

✳ That psychedelics have the potential to be amazing, fascinating medicines that feed our souls and inspire our spirits.
✳ That the benefits of these experiences could be just the medicine our species needs.
✳ That we could live in a culture which nurtures settings in which the self-administered and autonomously interpreted psychedelic experience is open to all who seek it.

And to realise this possibility we know that in many ways, and many places, there is work to be done.

We are living in a time of increased licensed research and I'm deeply appreciative of the work of organisations such as the Beckley Foundation, MAPS, The Tyringham institute and others for their herculean efforts. But their work is hampered by both the laws and culture surrounding the prohibition of these substances. Both things that need to change.

As things are now we know that the law relating to psychedelics is critical to our story. Most of us here, I would conjecture, took our first psychedelics in unlicensed and therefore possibly criminal circumstances. Given the severity with which some states punish the use of psychedelic sacraments, but for the Grace of God, we are all potentially the prisoners of prohibition.

For some people prohibition hits hard. I mentioned the chickens in my garden as an aside in an email to Leonard Pickard, who is in jail (serving two life sentences) for LSD manufacture. He told me in his reply that he'd not seen any creatures, besides humans, for 17 years. This is the real horror, the real bad trip—as we speak Leonard is shut away in his prison and we ourselves are only part-way free. So we must use all the strategies we have to transform this situation, even as these sacraments we have taken have changed us.

As a community of practice, we share our insights at gatherings such as this conference. Inspired, respectful and considerate of the teachings of contemporary indigenous psychedelic cultures, and informed by the discoveries of licensed and underground researchers.

We have a tremendous opportunity in this, the psychedelic renaissance. By sharing our collective wisdom I hope that we can build a culture suitable for a post-prohibition psychedelically upgraded world. More intelligent, more creative, more humane, more curious than perhaps ever before. Because, while it's easy to get Messianic about drugs, we could really be onto something here.

Perhaps these substances really are that powerful, that important to our species. These are medicines for the mind and therefore for our culture, and we should not be afraid to use them.

Through deploying psychedelic ceremony we are learning to make our own medicine. 'The medicine' as a whole is the

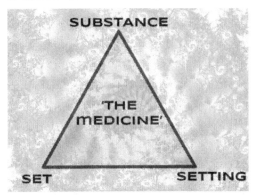

combination of the psychedelic experience within a set and setting designed to enhance its transformative and entheogenic potential. The medicine is the complete psychedelic triangle of set, setting and substance.

Ceremony does not necessarily imply orthodoxy and I would like to see us maintain a variety of psychedelic spaces in our culture; spaces for psychedelics as legitimate tools for healing, for research, for spiritual and for recreational use. For there are many medicines and no one prescription is right for everyone.

The medicine of psychedelic ceremony can heal our souls by providing opportunities for revelation, rapture and fun. Used as medicines these substances offer opportunities to transcend our limitations, to problem solve, to heal, to resolve conflict, to dispel the illusion of separation. Psychedelics employed in this manner can support our human search for meaning in a way predicated on personal spiritual inquiry rather than rote doctrine of any stripe. These are substances that entwine the scientific and the sacred, the religious and recreational, substances that can help make us whole.

With our wounded cultures and ecocidal behaviours it is clear that some wholeness and healing would not go amiss.

We could do with this good medicine.

Stay high and stay free!

Magick—Contains Mild Peril

Challenging our habitual selves.

Sometimes we find ourselves in dangerous and difficult situations. From illnesses that may develop inside us, to threats from violent outside forces. These situations shake us up, both literally and metaphorically. Then we may experience times of repose, peace and ease. Between these imagined extremes there is the range of psychic states and circumstances that we inhabit. Looked at from the perspective of our life-stories these ups and downs, these turnings of the Wheel of Fortune, may perhaps make us suspicious of concepts such as 'altered states of awareness' since that idea assumes a 'normal' state of awareness. In reality our 'I' is always in a state of flux and exists in a particular, ongoing, context.

Systems such as religion exist, in part, to provide us with psychic assistance as we encounter the slings and arrows of outrageous Fortune. There is now a strong body of research to suggest that spirituality itself can provide a protective function in terms of individual mental health.

A simple example is the use of death/rebirth motifs, for instance as part of formal initiation ceremony. We act 'as if'—as Austin Spare and philosopher Hans Vaihinger would put it—we are facing the actual and inevitable moment of our death.

Doing this kind of ritual, where we mimic the actual travails of life is what I like to call (in homage to the bonkers British certification system for films) the gnosis of 'mild peril'. Sadly this charming phrase 'contains mild peril' has now been dropped by censors because, following consumer research, it turned out to be rather esoteric, with only the British Board of Film Classification examiners knowing what it meant.

Mild peril; be it the point of the sword placed against the chest during a Wiccan or Masonic initiation, or the heat that one endures in the sweat lodge, is an important part of many occult practices. Part of the skill of the practitioner, especially if they are working in a group setting, is to create a ceremony where there is tension, difficulty, and after the ordeal, resolution and empowerment. Sometimes mild peril rites may be static (one might for example undertake an all-night vigil, outside in a remote power spot), or active (one might for instance spin, whirling dervish style, until trance and/or exhaustion is achieved). Mild peril, like safe, sane and consensual erotic play needs to be carefully approached so that while there is risk, it is managed intelligently.

For those of us who are engaged with esoteric practice the use of mild peril is important stuff. While we may perform rituals that are all about nurturing and supporting ourselves we also need to challenge ourselves too if we are to genuinely engage in the Great Work. One key function of mild peril is that it shakes us out of our complacent and repetitive behaviours. We all have these 'programs' within the construct of who we are, and that's not a bad thing in itself. Much of who we are is this repeated series of automatic routines that run with little or no conscious intervention, from the movement of food through our guts to the way we behave in certain social situations. However, we also need ways of breaking out of these patterns, especially if we want to understand ourselves from a new vantage point. Failing to do so reduces us to a simple stimulus-response pattern of action. We become creatures rather the Sphex wasp from *Mechanical Man* by Dean Wooldridge quoted in Douglas R Hofstadter's classic *Gödel, Escher, Bach*:

> *When the time comes for egg laying, the wasp Sphex builds a burrow for the purpose and seeks out a cricket which she stings in such a way as to paralyze but not kill it. She drags the cricket into the burrow, lays her eggs alongside, closes the burrow, then flies away, never to return. In due course, the eggs hatch and the wasp grubs feed off the paralyzed cricket, which has not decayed, having been kept in the wasp equivalent of a deep freeze. To the human mind, such an elaborately organized and seemingly purposeful routine conveys a convincing flavour of logic and thoughtfulness- until more details are examined. For example, the wasp's routine is to bring the paralyzed cricket to the burrow, leave*

it on the threshold, go inside to see that all is well, emerge, and then drag the cricket in. If the cricket is moved a few inches away while the wasp is inside making her preliminary inspection, the wasp, on emerging from the burrow, will bring the cricket back to the threshold, but not inside, and will then repeat the preparatory procedure of entering the burrow to see that everything is alright. If again the cricket is removed a few inches while the wasp is inside, once again she will move the cricket up to the threshold and re-enter the burrow for a final check. The wasp never thinks of pulling the cricket straight in.

On one occasion this procedure was repeated forty times, always with the same result.

Humans all too easily become trapped into Sphex-ish behaviours; addictions, thoughtless patterns of behaviour, ranting away on the internet about their tiresome obsessions—repeating activities less like an autonomous person and more like an automaton or a broken record. In these circumstances it may be very hard for the individual to find a way out of their behavioural loop. Luckily as a social species we may have others to help us. People with friends and, for folk in more difficult circumstances, support workers, healers or mental health professionals can help us snap out of Sphex-ish behaviours.

In a magical context the performance of practices as simple as ritual purification (ceremonial bathing for example) or as dramatic as Sun Dance endurance ordeals are all ways of changing our Set and Setting. The use of mild peril, where the blood is set pumping, adrenaline levels spike and we become hyper alert can, if properly managed, be a great way to break those patterns that can trap us in a Groundhog Day of repeated pointlessness. This way, unlike the Sphex wasp, we don't get flummoxed by our cricket being moved and instead break out of the tedious routine game and into something richer and more rewarding.

The Art of Witchcraft

An essay produced for the Chaos Magick Group Codex Chaotica *on the relationship between witchcraft and art.*

The word 'witch' is a spider. A signifier that weaves connections between many wild ideas. Her web is anchored to the curious and dark places in culture; the sexuality of women and of the queer; trafficking with denizens of the unseen and shamanic-spiritualist mediumistic trance, the folklore of healing and harming, the naked radical Masonic Mystery cult of Wicca and much more. As we widen our field of vision we notice that this web is drawn tight across still darker cultural space; the blackmailing practices of cunning folk (offering 'blessings', for a fee, to defend against imagined maleficia), the howling of Temperance Lloyd and her Sisters (hanged for the crime of witchcraft in a late 17th century England that should have known better), to southeast Africa, and the Malawi state courts (calling children in to testify that women kidnap them during the night and try to turn them into witches)...

There is the witchcraft of the Christian fundamentalist, the radical activist, the solitary kitchen crafter, the satanic eye-lined youth, the rotund working-class pagan, the datura smoking demonologist, the nervous Ouija-playing teenager, that odd-looking old lady who lives in the spooky run-down house on the edge of the town.

But our spider's web isn't a random mess; there is an underlying structure here however variable in its details. Each cobweb is unique, but we can trace something of the archetypal form of the witch through her many guises. An incomplete list of these motifs might run thus:

* Witchcraft is about women.
* Witchcraft is about the hidden, the occult, and the dark.
* Witchcraft is both beautiful and monstrous.
* Witchcraft is dangerous.
* Witchcraft is about sexual extremes; all or nothing.

For the vast majority of culture and history, the word 'witch' (or the equivalent term in other languages) suggested a worker of maleficent magic. Attempts by Wiccan and other contemporary Craft practitioners to find 'positive' uses of the term are legion and there are some good examples. The usual argument is that witchcraft is the 'dark' magic that has been oppressed by our patriarchal culture and therefore considered to be evil. There is perhaps some merit in this, if nothing else the tropes identified above are clearly connected with women, and more broadly common cultural notions of the oppressed feminine. The modern vocabulary of witchcraft challenges the simplistic reading of witchcraft as evil and turns this on its head; the malevolent cursing crones of former times become re-imagined as denigrated but beneficial midwives and healers.

Two women by Austin Osman Spare from Images & Oracles of Austin Osman Spare

For modern apologists of this pre-industrial witchcraft, the witch may not be all bad, but she isn't best pleased with our current phallogocentric society either. She may stride onto our cultural stage demanding her rights and, with her sisters, link arms to bar the way of lorries transporting atomic weapons. Perhaps that's one reason people get so cross when, instead of arising from the excluded darkness of women's discourse to change the world, she seems instead only interested in changing her name to that of a garden herb and baking organic cookies for family-friendly Sabbat celebrations. But maybe she'd make us angry whatever she did; whether she incarnates as Anton LaVey's 'Satanic Witch' or a stay-at-home Pagan Mom. That's part of the point about the witch, she disturbs, she challenges the way things should be and whether she calls herself Wiccan or not, spitting our hatred upon her is part of an ancient ritual. We reject her, she is wrong, too old, too young, too soft, too hard—she makes us uncomfortable, mixes things up, sweeps away certainty and replaces it with shadowy superstition and weird uncomfortable feelings. She is the scapegoat for whatever our culture fears.

My own engagement with witchcraft (which I've written about in more detail in *Magick Works* and *The Book of Baphomet*) is that it was one of the first forms of occultism I encountered in the flesh. This was during the 1980s where The Craft represented one of the most accessible, and to my mind evocative, arenas for group magical practice. Since that time, I've worked in eclectic experimental coven settings, Alexandrian and Gardnerian lineages and within so-called 'Traditional' witchcraft groups. Moreover, as I suspect anyone who spends time engaging with witchcraft will discover, there isn't necessarily much difference between the ritual technology and often the actual personnel involved in these variants of The Craft. While less experienced practitioners expend plenty of energy focusing on the 'narcissism of minor differences' (between 'traditions'), actual witches cheerfully incorporate whatever works into their system. Gardnerian Craft absorbs naturism and Freemasonry, Alexandrian Craft employs Qabalah, Feri Craft adopts Yezidi iconography, Sabbatic Craft is deeply indebted to the work of artist magician Austin Spare. Actual witches tend to blend all the above together (and more besides) into the cauldron of their practice.

Austin Osman Spare is also an inspiration to that other style of magick that incorporates whatever works; chaos magic. While Peter J. Carroll namechecks Spare in his work, Carroll's scientific style is perhaps less suited to engaging with the Spare material than it is with much of Crowley's work (he being the other tutelary spirit of chaos magic).

Possible image of Spare's Witch Mother *from his* The Focus of Life

Spare was undoubtedly a summoner of spirits. In the mode of the burgeoning spiritualist movement Spare had his own inner-world guides such as the Native American 'Black Eagle' as well as a host of 'familiars' with which he consorted (as well as lots of physical cats which he cared for in his home). For me, Spare is the link between the contemporary occult approach known as chaos magic and that mysterious spider-word that straddles many worlds; 'witchcraft'. And, as with pretty much every male witch before or since, it was a woman who brought Spare into The Craft.

Not much is known about Mrs Paterson, 'the witch Paterson' as her pupil Austin Spare titled her (sometimes spelt 'Patterson'). Images of her appear in his art and while historical evidence for Mrs P. as a corporeal human is scant, there is no doubt that she was a mythic reality for Spare.

The limited details that Spare provided (filtered through the lens of Kenneth Grant) are that Mrs Paterson came from a line of Salem witches that Cotton Mather had failed to eradicate. She was a fortune teller, and there is a suggestion that while she was unversed in the linguistic complexities and esoteric vocabulary that Spare employed, she was able to explain the most abstract of ideas with great ease. In this sense she is the archetypal witch; unlettered, untutored, and yet possessing the simple brilliance of the Noble Savage or imagined folk-wisdom of the working classes. (Witches are, commonly, neither particularly cultured nor monetarily wealthy individuals).

Mrs Paterson's abilities included the classic early spiritualist skill of conjuring things to visible appearance. When performing divinations she would externalise an idea, an event, a prophecy, into a darkened corner of the room so that the querent could quite literally see what she was thinking.

Yet for all her rough style the witch Paterson was, according to Grant, the figure from whom Spare derived his 'sex-magical formulae' for she was also 'a Delphic Pythoness'. One of these formulae (and again this is according to Grant, who is known to have put his own unique spin onto the Spare material—see for example the letters between him and Spare in *Zos Speaks!*) was the use of the earthenware virgin. This technique, briefly, consists of making a vessel suitable for a male to masturbate into in order to charge a sigil.

A frequent theme in Spare's work is that of transformation; humans into animals, animals into spirits, gods into sigilised script and so on. Paterson herself was able to shape-shift; becoming a haggard old woman or a nubile maiden as she desired. Grant says of Spare:

> *It amounted almost to an obsession with him and its origin lay in the fantastic transmogrification which, as a child, he had witnessed in Mrs Paterson. The wrinkled crone had appeared to change into a large-limbed voluptuous girl.*

(Grant's phraseology links Spare's iconic female with Crowley's "... magnificent beasts of women with large limbs, and fire and light in their eyes'" mentioned in *The Book of the Law.*)

Spare claimed to have been seduced by Mrs Paterson and that she was one of the figures with whom he travelled to the witches' Sabbat where all the usual lycanthropic and ecstatic stuff went down. While sometimes describing her as his 'Second Mother' the erotic relationship between her and Spare is not so much about incest as is about power of 'the older woman'. Mrs Patterson is the mature, perhaps postmenopausal, sexual initiator of our young sorcerer. She is the original Dark Satanic MILF.

Image of the waning moon and female figures by Austin Osman Spare in The Focus of Life

Marcus M Jungkurth in *Austin Osman Spare, Artist, Occultist, Sensualist,* provides a masterful psychological analysis of this process:

Spare's night-journey to the Witches' Sabbath led him to encounters not only with satyrs, ancient creatures and demons, but most notably with the dark side of the Great Mother ... The symbolic reality of the terrifying female draws its images mainly from the interior world, the negative elementary character of the female expresses itself in fantastic and chimerical images which do not originate in the outside world. Thus is becomes evident that the terrifying or monstrous female is a symbol of the unconscious itself. As Erich Neumann (The Great Mother, 1991) has shown, the experience of the negative or evil side of the anima is part of the mystery of inner transformation by the annihilation of the male or patriarchal consciousness and the subsequent reincarnation out of the female womb. Again the motif of reduction or regression shines through, here by reaching backwards to the cellular level of the very beginning of life itself. A destruction of traditional values occurs during this process, the ideals of beauty and harmony which are too often but a by-product of society's current tastes, are turned upside down in order to release the anima or female within: "The desertion of the 'Universal Woman' lying barren on the parapet of the Subconscious in humanity; and humanity sinking into the pit of conventionality. Hail! The convention of the age is nearing its limit, and with it a resurrection of the Primitive Woman". (Earth Inferno, 1905) His identification of the 'Universal Woman'——the mediatrix of the unknown acting as psychopompos——with the element of Earth underlines the dark aspect of his anima, her relation to death, decay and age, as the caverns of earth even in ancient times were both temples of initiation and tombs: the Great Mother taking all back into her what had originally emerged of her. Spare's encounters with his 'Universal Woman', the luring quintessence of desire, with whom he "strayed into the path direct", led to the formulation of 'The new sexuality of ZOS', a sexuality not being limited to mere sensuality, but

*defined as pure cosmic consciousness embracing reality,
freed from all convention and condition. For Spare, this
woman, of whom actual woman was but an incomplete and
distorted image, symbolized "all otherness", and to unite
with her would lead to the realization and attainment of the
Self.*

I hadn't planned to work with Mrs Paterson, though I was
familiar with the stories about her. I'd been at a ritual a year
or so previously where a group of us invoked Mrs Paterson
into the bodies of several women in our circle. The Brother
who led the ritual had himself worked with Mrs P. creating
an excellent puja style practice to summon her. I contacted
him when I commenced my own work and he gave me a few
tips:

"Ahhh YES, what are the details? I love Mrs Paterson, she
loves Sherry, boiled sweets, fudge, tea with milk and sugar
and sexual tension..."

My magical sibling also provided me with a soundscape
he'd created for working with her that I incorporated into
several rituals of my own.

Like I said I hadn't planned to begin a sequence of work
with Mrs Paterson. In fact, according to my online diary (via
the miracle of Facebook on a page called '#100MagicDays'
curated by Saddie LaMort) I'd just been doing some work with
the Goddess Eris (randomly selected from the *Portals of
Chaos* by Peter J. Carroll & Matt Kaybryn). Into the space
created by the Golden Apple of Discord came the witch.
Perhaps that's because for me 'the fairest' is indeed this witch-
woman (or perhaps it's totally random...) Anyhow my first
experiment was pretty simple. I used a soundscape I'd created
some years previously called 'Come to the Sabbat' plus a
strong dose of damiana tea. Prepared the space, vocalised my
intentions and then lay back and entered the dream world.

Naturally, being a powerful magician, I should now go on
at extraordinary length about the sexy/cool/weird journey to
the witches' Sabbat I experienced. In fact, I remembered little
of my dreams; tiny snatches of childhood stuff, someone
singing, and searching for a lost object.

What happened instead was that I started to produce art.

Turbulent Mother—Composition with pornography and river mud

I started to get a sense of some experiments I wanted to make. Digital artworks, or paintings, collages, drawings and few sculptural pieces, concerning the nature of the erotic. They explore, for example, how far one can morph a pornographic image until it stops being rude. Is that an abstract design or two figures fucking? Some of this art also seeks to look at the relationship between sexuality and identity. Some pieces are more clearly 'spells' that use erotic iconography (particular fetishized materials and objects) to launch specific ensigilised desires (usually as long-term, broad enchantments).

This new wave of my own art made use of cut-up techniques, overlaid images and drew on my experience of working in a museum to create sculptural works in boxes; styled to look like the strange exhibits one might encounter in the Boscastle Museum of Witchcraft & Magic. As well as decoupage from porn magazines, there were specimen pins, a female figure made from clay harvested from a local beach after a big storm, bones, keys, fishnet stockings, and magical inscriptions.

Exhibit 81—Composition with river mud, found clay, pornography
& Theban Script.

I paid particular attention to my dreams during this period and, unusually for me, recalled quite a lot of material. Some (as the ancient Greeks used to say) came through the gates of ivory but mostly they appeared through the gates of horn—that is they were 'true' dreams; not great prophetic teachings (at least not yet) but a few good psychological insights into myself and others, plus a few (retrospectively) tiny precognitive flashes (though not of any world-shattering helpfulness to me; I keep working to divine those six lottery numbers...). But the main treasure harvested from these dreams was inspiration for my artistic practice.

Damiana was a herb I used several times over this period, and along with this *Salvia divinorum*. In this instance I took the salvia by chewing the dried leaf. Having first thoroughly cleaned my teeth and washed out my mouth with alcohol (to enhance the absorption of the drug). I took this sacrament in what I think is by far the best situation; alone in silent darkness. The Mazatec people describe the salvia spirit as being like 'an elusive deer in the forest'. Chewed fresh leaves or masticated dry ones feel much the same. The trance is in some senses, subtle. You need to listen to what the salvia spirit says. Open your eyes, move about and (depending of course on how much and how long you've been chewing), the room is a bit spinney and you feel slightly drunk but nothing more remarkable. But close those eyes, lie back, and enter the darkness and watch how the organic-ketamine style visions unfold in ultra-violets, deep beetle-back blues and matrix-code greens. There are images too, fully formed pictures as may manifest with ayahuasca. Then slip from these visions into sleep where yet more visions may arise.

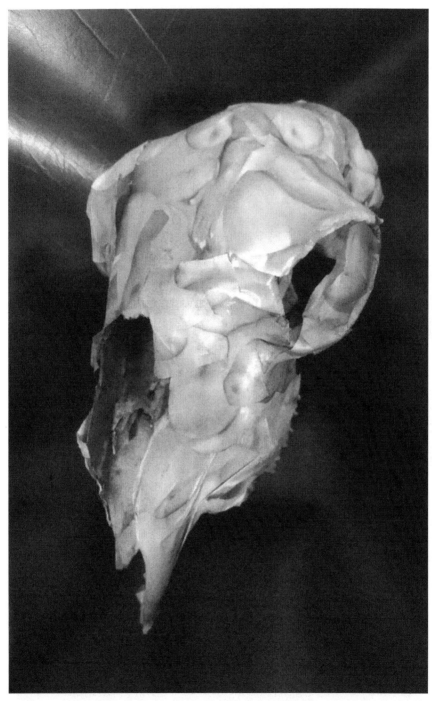

Sex and Death II—Composition with pornography and sheep skull

As I write this, the September Equinox has passed, and the leaves are being torn from the trees. The shops are dressed with broomsticks and pumpkin lanterns. My dreams are haunted by the witch and she currently seeks manifestation in the art I'm creating. As the darkness of the year rises and Halloween approaches, I prepare for the witches' Sabbat. There are black candles, boiled sweets and sherry with which to call Her to visible appearance.

The Work continues.

With thanks to:

> Frater Elijah
> Apokaliptikon Art
> Matthew Levi Stevens

References

Portals of Chaos by Peter J. Carroll & Matt Kaybryn, 2014.

Images & Oracles of Austin Osman Spare, Kenneth Grant, 1975.

The Magical Revival, Kenneth Grant, 1972.

Zos Speaks!: Encounters with Austin Osman Spare, Kenneth & Steffi Grant, 1998.

Neither-Neither: Austin Osman Spare and the Underworld, Marcus M. Jungkurth. First published in *Austin Osman Spare, Artist, Occultist, Sensualist*, 1999.

Magick Works, Julian Vayne, 2008.

The Book of Baphomet, Nikki Wyrd & Julian Vayne, 2012.

The Focus of Life, Austin Osman Spare, 1921.

The Magic of St Nectan's Glen

Following the first retreat that Nikki Wyrd and I ran at St Nectan's Glen, I wrote this article for Pagan Dawn magazine.

It was a few days after Beltane that I found myself walking, with my wizard's staff, through a valley in North Cornwall towards a sacred site that has been a place of pilgrimage for many generations. Through the valley flows the river Trevillet, known in Cornish as the Duwy, meaning 'dark river'. The name is apposite; though the water playfully cascades over the rocks on its way to the nearby Atlantic, it flows over the dark slate bedrock, of that deep, wooded valley. At May-time the leaves are bursting into bloom, the bluebells shimmer like an electric haze of colour beneath the new growth. By the height of summer the canopy leaves will have unfurled and the sparkling river will be cradled beneath deep green shadows.

The place is St Nectan's Glen, between Tintagel (famous as the birthplace of King Arthur and the site of Merlin's Cave) and Boscastle (home of the Museum of Witchcraft & Magic). I often come to the Glen. My first visit was perhaps a decade ago, not long after I moved to the West Country and, with only a vague notion of what was there, I was astonished when I finally reached the Kieve. The Kieve, the Cornish word for 'tub' or 'cup', is a space carved by the river as it drops 60 feet (18 metres), creating a waterfall that exits through a naturally made circle in the rock. The crashing water sings, creating rainbows in its spray. It spills from the bowl of the kieve, emptying into a wide, usually shallow, pool before flowing on towards Rocky Valley (another amazing place, featuring two labyrinth rock carvings of uncertain age, more waterfalls and further majestic landscape).

The largest waterfall of St Nectan's Glen is in fact only one of three falls (The Fairy Fall, as its name suggests, is delicate and mysterious whereas the Secret Fall is, well...). The

Glen is designated as being of Site of Special Scientific Interest; its damp shade supporting colonies of rare mosses and liverworts. There are also colonies of dippers which, unlike most songbirds, can swim underwater. Recently I'm also pleased to say that over 4,000 trees of many native species have been planted on what was previously rough grazing land adjacent to The Glen. At night the place is alive with owls, and bats, in the day there is scurrying in the leaf litter, the calling of hawks and ravens in the sky.

Nikki and me at St Nectan's Glen
(Photograph courtesy of Ciara Sherlock.)

Climbing the stone steps of The Glen, towards the ancient buildings (including a rock-hewn cell in which St Nectan— an Irish-born saint from Wales who did a good line in miraculous stuff—used to meditate) I pause for a moment. And remember...

The second time I came to The Glen was for a Samhain ritual maybe six years ago, along with my two children. This was to be one of those delightful family friendly Pagan ceremonies facilitated by Nicola Clare-Lydon and Peter Pracownik. Nicola and Peter (who are now firm friends) are visionary artists (they run a Gallery in Tintagel, Another Green World). If people ask me to describe Peter's art I tell them to imagine one of those tobacco tins you see in headshops with a picture of a dragon on it. Chances are that the dragon was painted by Peter. My second visit wasn't long after the Glen had been up for sale and purchased by a new owner. Naturally with such a magical place there had been concerns about who would purchase the site. What if it ended up like some horrid Disneyfied visitor attraction? But the magic of this landscape is strong, and the new and current owner is, quite literally, one of the good guys.

Over the years I've had many opportunities to do ceremony in this place. With Nicola in her role as Priestess of Glen I've turned the wheel of the year, sometimes as part of a circle with forty or more people. We meet together in the Kieve, standing in the shallow pool downstream of the cascading fall. The central altar is carefully constructed thing, a table standing on a platform of river stones. We call in the spirits, raising our words over the sound of rushing water. We've made magical fires (casting gunpowder on glowing charcoals within a cauldron), seen Handfastings and cast spells in the Kieve. This is our place.

But this place is not only ours, it's there to be shared and that's what I was helping to do as I walked towards The Glen with my staff.

When I was a young man I did, I have to admit, sometimes affect a wizard's staff. But for many years I hadn't bothered. But this time was different. I had my staff because I was one of 18 pilgrims, making their way to The Glen for the first residential retreat on the site.

My partner Nikki Wyrd would be facilitating the retreat too and this was to be the realization of a dream. We'd spent several years working with the current owners to develop the project. The current guardian wants to share 'the spirituality, the ecology and the history' of St Nectan's. The opportunity for people to stay there is another dimension of that mission. Numbers are limited, if nothing else by the fact that there is no way to drive to St Nectan's Glen (unless you have a four-wheel drive vehicle and have agreed access in advance). Pilgrims, like me, have to walk; though I'm pleased to say a Land Rover was provided to carry my gear up the hill (ceremonial drum, sage for smudging, ritual robes, a badger skull... that sort of thing).

Nearing the top of the steps, supported by my trusty staff—a gift many years previous from a magician in New Zealand—I see my friends. The people that work at the Glen are all local folk, many of whom I have stood alongside in ceremony in the Kieve. They are my family, my tribe, and the fact that I am able to do my work with this magical place with these good people inspires me to give thanks.

Guided by my staff I descend the stone steps towards the waterfall, down again into the darkness and the sound of rushing water. Past the great beech trees, the luxuriant ferns and great crags, down to where the offerings are made.

In common with many sacred sites the world over, here at St Nectan's Glen people leave offerings. These are habitually ribbons hung from trees. In the breeze the many colours announce the fact that humans, for many different reasons, are choosing to respond to this magical place by decorating it. The staff at the Glen pay close attention to the offerings, encouraging the use of biodegradable materials, and sensitively removing some of the ribbons at the end of each season (and burying them with suitable blessings). For my part, I hung a ribbon on one of the trees a few years back in memory of my Dad. This time I don't need to leave anything physical, but I am moved to sing.

Leaning my staff upon a rock, I walk barefoot into the water. A little further out and there She is (those of us who work magic at this site simply call the large waterfall 'She'). I raise my hands and sing the word 'awen', charm of inspiration, hoping that I can be inspired to do my best to share the magic of this place with the people who will be at this, and many other retreats. I dip my hand in the water, place some on my forehead, place my hands together and bow. She is quite magnificent.

I gently sing a verse from the Song of St Nectan's Glen...

Across the land,
Down to the sea,
O waterfall,
Fall through me.

Water fall, fall, fall,
Water fall, fall, fall,
Water fall, fall, fall,
Through me.

The Blessings hang,
Upon the tree,
O waterfall,
Fall through me.

Water fall, fall, fall,
Water fall, fall, fall,
Water fall, fall, fall,
Through me.

And now She flows
So strong and free
O waterfall,
Fall through me.

Water fall, fall, fall,
Water fall, fall, fall,
Water fall, fall, fall,
Through me.

Back on shore I dry off, taking up my pilgrim staff. Nikki had asked each person attending our retreat to bring a staff since they are going on a pilgrimage. Like all good symbolism this works on many levels. A staff is really useful in the steep and rocky terrane of St Nectan's Glen. I notice that, having been fortunate to have lived for nearly half a century, my wizard's staff is no longer an affectation but has been transformed into a real source of strength and support.

I climb back up the steps. The day is alive with birdsong, a robin (for me a sign of my Dad's spirit) boldly pecks seed at the feet of a cat (a sculpture of the Goddess Bast that stands guard at the entrance the waterfall). I give thanks to the Great Spirit for this opportunity, and for all those who care for, and share, and are inspired by this sacred place.

As I walk up the road, ready to greet the retreat participants, the daytime pilgrims are leaving. Twilight will be here soon and our group will be alone. At our night-time ritual we chant incantations over a vessel of sacred water, and set our intentions for the weekend.

The next morning we ceremonially take the magical water on a tour of the site intending to eventually reunite it with that flowing through the Kieve. We visit the Guardian Tree, then new Fire Pit, where we plan (the next day) to light the first ceremonial fire.

It is around noon as our chalice carrying group carefully descend into the Kieve, to find that some daytime pilgrims are already there. But there isn't any conflict or competition for the space; these two visitors are doing another common ritual practice at the site; with stones from the riverbed they are hammering silver coins into a huge log. The log lays half in the water looking like a dragon covered with thousands of coin scales. We are just the latest in the line of pilgrims visiting this place to make offerings. We arrive for our ceremony just as these early daytime pilgrims are finishing theirs.

Once each of us has scattered some drops from the Chalice into the waters, one of our group (an Alexandrian High Priestess) bears our ritual cup into the heart of the Kieve. The water we have blessed streams down into the foam. She bravely presses the cup into the powerful waterfall. The cup is filled again and emptied once more. We sing the word 'awen', to honour Her.

As we turn to go, more daytime visitors are turning up, and it's all good. Their top hats stuck with feathers, tattoos and jewellery indicate that these folk know what's what, we smile and nod to each other. Our group heads back to the private space of the retreat buildings. We're just another ceremony, just another set of pilgrims passing through this sacred landscape.

I am honoured to be just another pilgrim in this magical land. Do please go and visit St Nectan's Glen if you have the opportunity, it really is quite magical.

Whether we connect with nature by going on retreat or simply for a wander in the woods. Whether we develop our relationship with landscape through psychogeography, cultivation (like coppicing or gardening) or adventurous exploration; what matters is that we seek those connections. These relationships, these experiences enrich us and in doing so benefit all the others around us.

May we each find our Way in this shared magical landscape.

Blessed Be!

Orange Sunshine

The magic of LSD.

The solstice is past, Christmas and the festival of the Unconquered Sun are done. Over the town fireworks burst like vast flaming dandelions against the cold night, and now the midnight revellers have returned to their homes.

Our home twinkles with tinsel, the tree in the corner of the room sparkles with fairy lights. Here, in the final phase of the Christmas season, we are in the time of liminal days. Days that, according to one story were gained for humanity by Thoth, who played a trick on Ra with a couple of loaded dice and a bet with the moon god Iah. These extra days stray beyond the 360 degrees of a circle, giving us a year of 365 days, comprising one complete solar orbit. It was during this period that the five major gods of Dynastic Ancient Egypt were born (Osiris, Isis, Set, Nephthys, and Horus).

If we cast our mythological eye further north, we see similar ideas about the days around midwinter as a period somehow outside the circles of time. In the Northern Hemisphere, Midwinter may be *the* pivotal period of the calendar; this is a time of stories and ghosts, of ancestors and new life, a time so dark that the best option is to stay inside, snug and warm and dreaming. Our annual calendar clicks on one number.

Into this in betweenness time it is our will to place our magical intentions, our hopes and resolutions for the New Year. In order to do this, and to discover new opportunities, connections and insights we are planning to hotwire our minds. To do this we have some LSD.

The acid comes with a sunburst logo printed in late 1960s style, and suitably gaudy colours on the blotter. A homage to the iconic Orange Sunshine acid produced by countercultural heroes Tim Scully and Nicholas Sand and distributed by The Brotherhood of Eternal Love (Peace be Upon Them). This acid is strong, at least by modern standards, I'd estimate around

300 µg per tab. We want to use the journey to help us find inspiration and plan our projects and so decide to do half a tab each. This should allow us to keep our focus on the session's intention while still achieving the parallel processing effect that LSD creates at a neurological level (by massively increasing the connectivity of previously discrete brain regions). We're also hoping that it will be fun.

The house is prepared with firewood for the hearth, washing up done and ourselves showered and bathed. Wearing clean comfortable clothes, we spend the evening chilling out. We want to take the acid through the night and, since dawn will not break until almost 9am, we wait until midnight before we begin the journey.

We stand together in the centre of the room. The medicine is prepared in a ceremonial bowl, the playlist and art supplies are near at hand. We begin by calling to the directions, turning to each cardinal point and asking, "May the doors of perception be cleansed". We place our hands on the earth 'May we be supported and nourished by the earth', and reaching up, 'May we be inspired and high as the stars above us!'

Sitting together we bless the medicine, those alchemists that create it and those medicine carriers that have brought it to us. The blotter paper tastes metallic, we chew for a while, and then swallow.

We begin with some positive dance music, a layering of warm sounds and up-tempo, undemanding beats. We draw, making plans and expressive artworks. We stretch and sit in meditation. At one point I venture out into the garden. The temperature has plummeted, and the clear sky is fierce with the brilliant points of stars. Orion leads Sirius into the sky of the wee hours, a shooting star flashes across the edge of the galaxy and I make a wish.

Later there is a period when the music stops. My partner expertly navigates her PC ready to play a favourite tripping album of mine, Steve Hillage's *Rainbow Dome Musick*. During the silent interlude the pattern making power of the medicine is such that the gentle hum of electrical equipment and the crackle of the fire are transformed into a textured drone composition.

We lay down together, embracing on the couch and I close my eyes. There is a vast whirling world within, replete with bizarre hyperreal images. As my observer self explores this territory I can feel the walls between concepts collapsing in on themselves. Previously discrete regions of my mind are blending, blurring, re-configuring and ejecting new forms into my inner vision. I can pick my way through this psychic wonderland, pausing to observe the more challenging content within my psyche. I'm able to watch with a detached interest how those blockages and problems are swept away by the endless mutability of thought and new perspectives on old issues. A carousel of concepts spins through me, expressed at a visual and visceral level. While I'm physically motionless there is a sense of movement in my body, as though I am rippling, spinning, growing somehow. I am indeed travelling without moving. My mind is wide open.

I focus my attention on the form of my lover beside me. The edges of 'me' slip away and I am left deliciously uncertain where I end and she begins. Though there is occasional polymorphous erotic imagery in these visions this sense of interpenetration isn't sexual in the typical sense. Rather than rising up kundalini style from the earth, this union cascades from a shared mindscape into a whole body somatic blending. I pay attention to this process, occasionally squeezing her hand gently as the love and shared identity I'm perceiving percolates down to the humble everyday fact of our mammalian bodies lying together.

The crackling of the fire startles me a couple of times. Acid brings us to attention and I enjoy the jolt of alertness which, under less supportive circumstances, might spiral into paranoia and the fear. I'm also enjoying the subtle feelings of megalomania that LSD can generate. I imagine the fabulous power of Pharaonic Egypt, the bright gold and lapis of the imperial temples. Eye of Horus shapes emerge in my drawings and gleaming hawks with wide stretched wings rise, justified and ancient, from the inner horizon of my mind.

Then it is time to do some magic.

There is a hypersigil, 23 years in the making, the magical work of the KLF, also known as the Justified Ancients of Mu Mu. 2017 marks the 23rd anniversary of Bill Drummond and Jimmy Cauty's incineration of one million pounds on the Isle of Jura and their self-imposed withdrawal from the music industry. On the first day of the New Year a film has been released onto the internet. It is titled "**KLF 01 01 2017 WTF FOUND VHS [unplayable on some mobile devices - VIEW ON PC/MAC/LINUX]**". The movie is an intense journey through KLF music videos, flashframe data, and an outstanding Wicker Man style ceremony complete with large numbers of robed participants and some very concerned looking journalists. Already the film contains many overlays, weird cut-ups and powerful imagery. The LSD we're on makes the screen into a magical portal, all the way back beyond ABBA to the ancient lost continent of Mu. After-images and acid tracers expand beyond the surface of the display and enter the room. This is a shocking, powerful download from Current 23.

We're past the peak now and gently gliding into land. We have some tea and continue to draw on large sheets of paper, recording the insights of the night.

In the morning we go into the garden. The world is spangled with frost. The ivy leaves are dusted hard with ice, the sky an intense, hard bright blue. The descendants of dinosaurs row through the air. Rooftops are white. The first rays of dawn reflect from the windows on the western side of the valley.

My partner makes us a breakfast of yogurt, berries and oranges. While she does this, I tidy the room we have spent the night in. I shake out the hearth rug, dust down the fire and light fresh incense. I open the curtains and the freezing sunshine overcomes the fairy lights.

We give thanks to the spirits of the place and the time and break our fast.

Gentle human-scale dub music sends us to our bed.

Outside, the dawn chorus sings on.

The Ace of Pentacles.
Designed for the Chaos Magic Group (CMG) tarot deck.

Printed in Great Britain
by Amazon